CHINA'S EMERGING NEW ECONOMY

The Internet and E-Commerce

John WONG

NAH Seok Ling

East Asian Institute
National University of Singapore

SINGAPORE UNIVERSITY PRESS
NATIONAL UNIVERSITY OF SINGAPORE

World Scientific
Singapore • New Jersey • London • Hong Kong

Published by

Singapore University Press
Yusof Ishak House, National University of Singapore
31 Lower Kent Ridge Road, Singapore 119078

and

World Scientific Publishing Co. Pte. Ltd.
P O Box 128, Farrer Road, Singapore 912805
USA office: Suite 1B, 1060 Main Street, River Edge, NJ 07661
UK office: 57 Shelton Street, Covent Garden, London WC2H 9HE

British Library Cataloguing-in-Publication Data
A catalogue record for this book is available from the British Library.

ISBN 981-02-4495-9 (pbk)

Printed in Singapore.

CONTENTS

THE NEW ECONOMY

Emergence of the New Economy

Moving into the 1990s, especially after Deng Xiaoping's tour of South China in the spring of 1992, China's rapid progress towards economic modernization and globalization has caught many observers by surprise. Deng's tour sparked off a new and bold phase of economic reform and open-door policy for China. The tour, in retrospect, was just a convenient occasion for him to prepare China for the so-called "socialist market economy" with radical reform measures. As a result, China experienced spectacular economic performance, with its economy growing at an average annual rate of 10.5% during 1991–99.

Rapid economic growth is usually accompanied by rapid structural change. Initially, structural change is manifested in the rise of manufacturing and services at the expense of agriculture. Towards the end of the 1990s, China's manufacturing sector itself was undergoing restructuring, with old, labour-intensive industries steadily giving way to new and more sophisticated activities. The same has happened to its service sector, as higher value-added service activities emerged, particularly in its modern metropolises like Shanghai, Beijing and Guangzhou. As a large and diverse economy, China can embrace and facilitate such a dual process of concurrent "development" and "transformation" with very little disruption. In other words, China can, on the one hand, promote labour-intensive industrialization in some areas and some sectors, and also push for faster industrial upgrading in other places and other sectors, on the other.

Accordingly, China's economy in recent years, despite its overall backwardness, has started to develop industries or activities which are broadly defined as components of the New Economy. In China, as elsewhere, its nascent New Economy has been driven by rapid globalization and the rise of information technology (IT), or rather, the increase in the digitalization of all information. (Table 1 highlights some distinctive features between the old and new economies.)

Indeed, China today is very much caught up in the relentless global process of the IT revolution. Ever since the reform and liberalization drive of the Chinese government, China's IT industry has been growing rapidly at about 30% annually[1] (Chart 1 shows the structure of China's IT industry).

In 1999 alone, total IT sales increased by 16.2% to reach 172 billion yuan (US$20.8 billion).[2] By the middle of 2000, the number of registered Internet users hit 16.9 million, of which 14% had tried e-commerce;[3] and its mobile phone population is already the second largest in the world,[4] amongst which 30% would be using Wireless

---

[1]"The Current Status & Future Prospects of China's Mobile Telecommunication", paper presented by Mo Y. J. at the Conference on China's WTO Accession and Its Impact on Northeast Asia (28–29 June 2000), Seoul, Korea. The event was organized by the Korea-China Economic Forum.

[2]"China IT Industry Sales Reached US$21 billion in 1999", *Chinaonline* (1 February 2000), http://www.chinaonline.com.

[3]"War on Net Hots Up", *South China Morning Post* (12 July 2000); and "E-commerce In China: The CCIDnet Survey", *CCIDnet.com* (27 April 2000), http://www.ccidnet.com.

[4]"Don't Stifle China's IT Revolution", *Asian Wall Street Journal* (28 February 2000) and "China Succeeds Japan As Largest Cellphone Market In Asia-Pacific Region", *China News Service* (22 August 2000).

Table 1. Features of the Old and New Economies

FEATURES	OLD ECONOMY	NEW ECONOMY
Overview		
Markets	Stable	Dynamic
Scope of competition	National	Global
Form of Organization	Hierarchical/Bureaucratic	Networked
Industry Specific		
Organization of production	Mass production	Flexible production
Key drivers of growth	Capital/Labour	Innovation/Knowledge
Key technology driver	Mechanization	Digitalization
Source of competitive Advantage	Lowering costs through economies of scale	Innovation, quality, time-to-market and cost
Importance of research/innovation	Low-moderate	High
Relations with other firms	Minimal	Alliances and collaboration
Workforce		
Policy goal	Full employment	Higher real wages and incomes
Skills	Job-specific skills	Broad skills and cross-training
Requisite education	A skill or degree	Lifelong learning
Labour-management Relations	Adversarial	Collaborative
Nature of employment	Stable	Marked by risk and opportunity
Government		
Business-Government Relations	Impose requirements	Encourages growth opportunities
Regulation	Command and control	Marked tools, flexibility

Source: The State New Economy Index, *The New Economy Index*, November 1998, http://www.neweconomyindex.org/.

Chart 1. Structure of China's Information Technology Industry

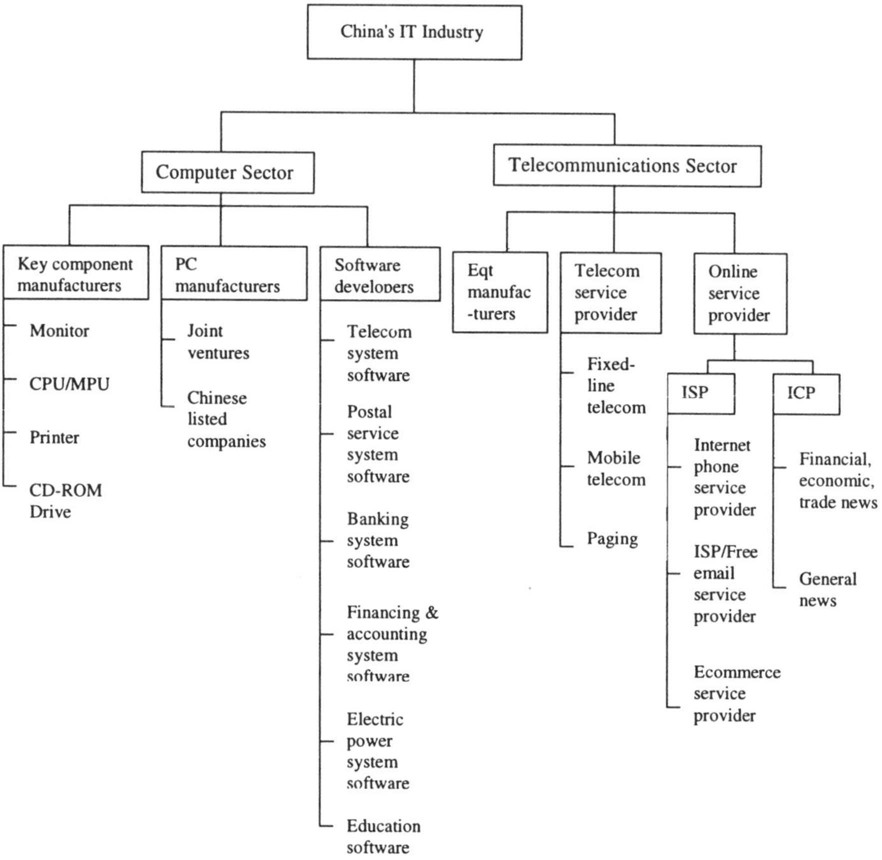

Source: "China's IT Industry", *Chinaonline* (July 2000), http://www.chinaonline.com.

Application Protocol (WAP), i.e. accessing the Internet via mobile phones. It is envisaged that the application of the latest IT technology such as Internet Protocol telephony and WAP will before long become a fairly common phenomenon in the daily lives of many urban Chinese.

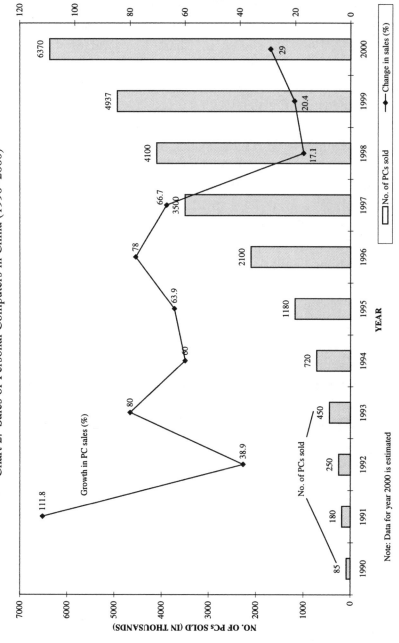

Chart 2. Sales of Personal Computers in China (1990–2000)

Note: Data for year 2000 is estimated

The rapid development of IT infrastructure in China in recent years has laid a good foundation for the emergence of its New Economy. In 1999, as shown in Chart 2, a total of 4.9 million personal computers (PCs) were sold in China. Furthermore, domestic computer hardware sales (accounting for 76% of total sales in the computer industry) registered a 13% rise over 1998 to reach 130 billion yuan while sales of software and information services products amounted to 41.5 billion yuan, registering a 27.5% increase.

At the same time, sales of telecommunications products reached about 100 billion yuan in 1999,[5] while total telecommunications business turnover grew 24% to hit 240 billion yuan in the same year.[6] China in 1999 had 110 million fixed line phone subscribers and 43 million mobile phone users.[7] (See Chart 3.) The mobile communications network can now cover 96% of China's counties and cities.[8] By the first half of 2000, the number of fixed-line and mobile phone subscribers increased another 15 million and 17 million to reach 125 million and 60 million, respectively.[9] China's telecom-munications sector has indeed grown by leaps and bounds.

In the meanwhile, China's IT products are expected to grow to 700 billion yuan, accounting for 8% of the country's total industrial output value by the end of 2000.[10] While China's computer market is expected to grow by 20% in 2000, with overall sales registering 205 billion yuan,[11] the market size of the hardware, software and

---

[5]*Ibid.*

[6]"China's Information Industry Booming in 1999", *Chinaonline* (1 February 2000), http://www.chinaonline.com.

[7]*Ibid.*

[8]*Ibid.*

[9]"China Telecom Announces Further Price Cuts", *South China Morning Post* (17 July 2000).

[10]"Boosting IT Industry to Meet World Trend", *China Daily* (4 June 1998).

[11]"China's Information Industry Booming in 1999", *Chinaonline* (1 February 2000), http://www.chinaonline.com.

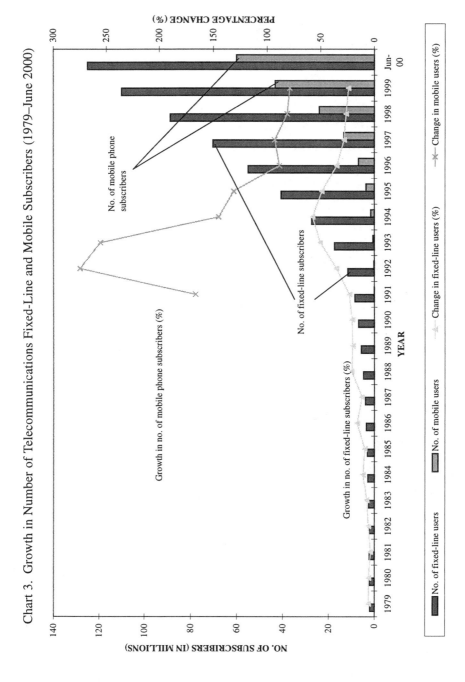

Chart 3. Growth in Number of Telecommunications Fixed-Line and Mobile Subscribers (1979–June 2000)

information services industries is expected to reach 151 billion yuan, 22.5 billion yuan and 31.5 billion yuan, respectively.[12]

To cap all this, China's overall high technology (hi-tech) exports increased by 25% to reach an estimated value of US$25 billion in 1999.[13] In fact, hi-tech items recorded the highest growth in China's overall exports. By the end of 2000, hi-tech exports are expected to reach US$30 billion, accounting for 15% of China's total exports.

The Internet and E-commerce as Driving Forces

Admittedly, the two main crucial driving forces behind the New Economy are the Internet and e-commerce. China has made a good start in both areas. The Chinese Internet industry is growing at an unprecedented rate compared to other sectors. In fact, since its debut in 1994, Internet subscribers grew exponentially from a mere 1,600 in 1994 to 2.1 million in 1998 and further to 8.9 million in 1999. (See Chart 4.) In mid-2000, the number of Chinese "netizens" (i.e. Internet users) soared to 16.9 million. By the end of 2000, China's Internet users may well exceed the original forecast of 20 million. Meanwhile, registered domains and websites have also been increasing at similarly high rates. In June 2000, there were over 99,000 registered domains and 27,000 websites in China.

These websites cover a wide range of fields. There are portals like Sina.com and Sohu.com; websites specializing in news such as eastern.net.cn and 21dnn.com; and websites specifically designed for medical care, tourism, electronics, transportation, fashion, employment and community services. These websites cover many

---

[12]"The General Development Situation of the Computer Market Between 1999–2000", *Eastwallstreet.com* (8 July 2000), http://international.yestock.com.
[13]"China Hi-tech Exports Increased by 25% in 1999", *China Securities* (12 January 2000).

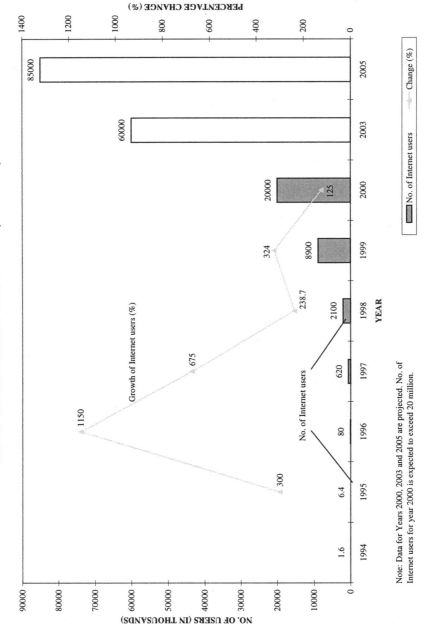

Chart 4. Growth of Internet Users in China (1994–2005)

Note: Data for Years 2000, 2003 and 2005 are projected. No. of Internet users for year 2000 is expected to exceed 20 million.

aspects of life. Entering the third wave of the Internet revolution, the Chinese people will soon find their life more colourful and their outlook broader.

The first wave of the Internet was characterized by the emergence of the first generation of netizens, the Internet Service Providers (ISPs), as represented by i.com.cn. Next came portals such as Sina.com, Sohu.com and Netease.com, boosting the popularity of the Internet. Currently, at the third wave of the Internet, China focuses on the spin-offs brought about by the Internet, by popularizing and extending the application of e-commerce or e-business. Various concept websites and commercial models such as business-to-consumer (B2C), business-to-business (B2B), consumer-to-consumer (C2C), business-to-business-to-consumer (B2B2C), business-to-consumer-to-business (B2C2B), consumer-to-business-to-consumer (C2B2C) and consumer-to-consumer-to-business (C2C2B) have emerged, with B2B being China's main development focus.

At present, China boasts over 1,100 e-commerce websites. E-commerce transactions in China registered a total revenue of 200 million yuan in 1999, or twice as much as in 1998.[14] Although B2C e-commerce, or online shopping alone, totalled only 55 million yuan in 1999, the estimated transaction volume in 2000 is 224 million yuan, a 300% increase from the previous year. Indeed, many of China's current 16.9 million netizens are potential online purchasers.

The boom of the Chinese cyber industry has naturally attracted the attention of foreign interests despite the government's existing ban on foreign involvement. Initially, Information Minister Wu Jichuan and some protectionist-minded officials had threatened to

---

[14]"MII Puts Out Its Own 1999 E-commerce Figures", *Chinaonline* (20 January 2000), http://www.chinaonline.com.

close the Internet sector to foreign investment. But the position has quickly changed once China decided to join the World Trade Organization (WTO), and Premier Zhu Rongji has now opened the Internet sector to 50% foreign ownership. Suffice to say that the Chinese government has come to realize that the Internet is totally different from traditional businesses that it had once tried to restrict. Zhu has also recognized the futility of restricting the Internet sector as the Internet companies do not need factories or plants to operate. Furthermore, they are borderless. The case in point is Sohu.com, one of China's top portals, which is based in Beijing but registered in Delaware.

At present, the Internet sector in China, on account of its explosive growth, can best be described as in a state of flux, which is also plagued by many structural shortcomings, as will be elaborated in the next chapter. The explosion of domestic websites is not backed by growth of actual output and revenues. The industry is actually entering into a consolidation phase, with many weak companies failing and fading away due to strong competition. It is estimated that about 80% of the country's Internet companies would close down in the near future, leaving the stronger portals to survive.[15] Those which eventually succeed will fuel the next-phase of expansion of China's IT-based New Economy.

Embracing the New Economy

The IT revolution presents China a good opportunity to propel itself into the New Economy. China's President Jiang Zemin has noted that the world is currently embracing a technology revolution, of which information and gene technology will feature more prominently. In particular, Jiang believes that e-commerce would

---

[15]"Vicissitude of the Internet", *Beijing Review* (31 July 2000).

be instrumental in the drive to develop China's economy and society. Eventually, traditional industries and information network would converge. In addition, China's Premier Zhu Rongji has pledged strong government support to enable the country to adapt itself to the "new situation of an information-based economy and the new challenge of global technological competition".[16] By embracing the New Economy, the Chinese government ultimately aims at achieving technology-driven economic growth. Zhu has also commented that "only when high technology (hi-tech) is developed, the phenomenon of a bubble economy can be avoided". Zhu also sees the IT sector as a catalyst for the restructuring of the old economy.[17]

In embracing the new economy and the rapid advancement of the hi-tech industry, the Chinese leaders have indicated their commitment to support and develop China's science and technology by promoting the strategy of "revitalizing the nation through science and education", popularly known as *Kejiao Xingguo* in Chinese. Under this strategy, a few initiatives have been identified, including: to universalize 9-year compulsory education for 80% of the population in various regions; to eliminate another 3 million illiterates; and to increase government investment in education by allocating 1% more of the government budget to education.[18]

At present, China has about 3 million people engaged in scientific and technological activities, of which 1.5 million are scientists and engineers. With a population of 1.2 billion, this number is obviously not sufficient to support the future needs of this vast country. Furthermore, R&D expenditure works out to be only a minuscule

---

[16]"Hi-tech Confucian Future", *South China Morning Post* (13 October 1999).

[17]"Information Development A Catalyst for Change", *South China Morning Post* (8 February 2000).

[18]CREC: China Education News Archive (18 March 1999), http://www.hku.hk/chinaed/chinaednews_index_bydate.htm.

0.7% of GDP. In addition, there is also the question of the suitable kind of science and technology (S&T) training experience for business and industrial development, i.e., the business and management aspects of S&T, or the so-called technopreneurial capability.

In a recent interview with the magazine *Science*, President Jiang Zemin acknowledged that between 1978 and 1999, nearly 320,000 Chinese students went abroad to study and of these, only 110,000 have returned to China. To tap this source of S&T manpower, China stepped up measures to attract Chinese S&T nationals overseas to return to work in China.[19] Recently, the Chinese government established a representative office in Silicon Valley with the objective of attracting mainland nationals who are working in hi-tech firms back to China. Various cities and regions in China have also come up with their own incentive measures to attract overseas Chinese students to return home to work.

At the same time, the government is nurturing various cities or regions into hi-tech zones to step up S&T development in the mainland. Accordingly, the *Zhongguancun* district of Beijing (China's equivalent of the Silicon Valley and the pioneer of China's IT industry with the first technology firms established here in 1981) was to spearhead the development of advanced technology for the New Economy. *Zhongguancun* will also play a key role in the country's economic reform programme in the first decade of the 21st century.[20]

In June 1999, a plan was formulated to speed up the technological development of *Zhongguancun*. The plan, approved by the State

---

[19]For many years, the Chinese government policy towards students studying overseas has been: supporting them to go abroad, encouraging them to return and allowing them to come and go freely.

[20]"Silicon Zone to Drive Reforms", *Hong Kong Standard* (12 October 1999).

Council, is for the establishment of the *Zhongguancun Science and Technology Park* (ZSTP). Under this plan, the ZSTP will be composed of Haidian Park, Fengtai Park, Changping Park, the Yizhuang Beijing Economic and Technological Development Area and Electronic City. The move marks China's search for a new stimulus to sustain its high growth while fulfilling its target of economic modernization by the mid-21st century.

Over the next 10 years, the ZSTP is slated to become a world-class scientific and technological zone with distinctive features of modern China. It will act as a comprehensive experimental base for promoting China's development through science and education and will serve as a base for:

- the demonstrations of national scientific and technological innovation;
- the application of scientific and technological results to production; and
- the cultivation of high-quality and innovative professionals.

Zhongguancun has since reported considerable breakthroughs in tapping human resources, pursuing new undertakings, providing intermediate and social services and establishing a capital market. It has started a venture capital system to meet the financing problem of the small and medium-sized enterprises. As a result of the State's preferential policies, the business environment of many new and hi-tech enterprises in *Zhongguancun* has greatly improved. In 1999, *Zhongguancun* registered more than 6,600 hi-tech enterprises.[21] Its combined industrial output value exceeded 50 billion yuan and the total revenue amounted to 86.4 billion yuan. For the first quarter of 2000, the total industrial output value and total profits increased

---

[21]"The New Beat of *Zhongguancun*", *Beijing Review* (24 July 2000).

by 32% and 75% respectively, compared to the same period last year.[22]

Aided by its knowledge-based ambience and the concentration of hi-tech activities, new enterprises are springing up everyday in *Zhongguancun*. Most of them are established by young scientists and technicians, with intellectual property rights of their own. Many of them are foreign-trained scientists and technologists, lured back by the government who has granted special incentives to attract overseas capital and talents (students and researchers studying or working abroad) to come back to *Zhongguancun*.

In short, the numerous Internet start-ups in *Zhongguancun*, coupled with the widespread application of IT products and government's efforts in promoting the IT sector, signify China's enthusiasm in embracing the New Economy.

Besides its drive to attract Chinese nationals to return to China, the government has also come up with other initiatives to boost its *Kejiao Xingguo* programme. The government has recognized the important role foreigners have played in developing the hi-tech sector in China (some 80% of the country's hi-tech exporters are foreign-invested enterprises). Hence, to entice foreign firms to develop the hi-tech sector, the State Council in 1999 started granting tax benefits to foreign invested firms (FIEs) for investing in technological projects. The tax benefits would allow FIEs which have increased their technological development by 10% in the previous year to deduct half of that year's technology spending from its taxable income.[23]

In its bid to boost hi-tech production and exports, the Chinese government has also pledged to encourage non-governmental venture

---

[22]*Ibid.*

[23]"China To Grant Foreign Invested Firms Hi Tech Tax Breaks", *Chinaonline* (19 October 1999), http://www.chinaonline.com.

capital inflow from both home and abroad. The government has set up a venture capital investment fund, targeting at hi-tech firms. It aims to attract "first-class" fund managers and specific foreign investment projects.

More specifically, the government recently drafted a broad range of financial incentives to boost the competitiveness of computer software and integrated-circuit companies. The State Council has mapped out new policies to encourage IT development, allowing Chinese firms to "raise creativity and competitiveness" on the world market. The policies are aimed to boost China's software and integrated circuit (IC) sectors so that the country's software development and production can meet or approach world standards. Under the new policies, the government welcomes venture capital in the IT industry, and the stocks held by venture investment companies can be traded on the market after listing on the stock exchange. Qualified companies will be entitled to a rebate of most of the 17% value-added tax.[24] New software firms will receive an income tax waiver for the first two years of recorded profits. For the subsequent three years, income tax will be reduced by half. Investments exceeding 8 billion yuan will receive tax incentives. Furthermore, the government will also give special support to the research and development of significant software technologies.[25]

IT firms with annual software export exceeding US$1 million will be accorded their own export rights.[26] Customs duties will also be reduced on certain imports. In fact, under the umbrella of the World Trade Organisation (WTO), China has agreed to eliminate

---

[24]"State Boost for Hi-tech", *South China Morning Post* (12 July 2000).
[25]"China Sets Out IT Development Policy", *South China Morning Post* (13 July 2000).
[26]*Ibid.*

all tariffs by 2005 on IT products such as computers, semiconductors and Internet-related equipment.[27]

For a developing economy like China's, which is still characterized by extensive backwardness, the rapid growth of its New Economy segment is rather astonishing. Despite its preoccupation with current efforts in dealing with the many pressing problems of economic reform and social changes, the Chinese government has not neglected the New Economy. What it has done to promote the New Economy, though still modest in real terms, has been quite impressive. Its open support and firm endorsement of the IT industry are in fact quite significant at the early stages of the development of the New Economy. According to some observers, China's IT industry, on account of its vast market potential and steady improvement, may one day overtake that of Taiwan, Singapore and Hong Kong.[28]

---

[27]"Don't Stifle China's IT Revolution", *Asian Wall Street Journal* (28 February 2000).

[28]"Mainland To Lead Region In Hi-tech Industries", *South China Morning Post* (12 July 2000).

THE INTERNET IN CHINA

Explosive Growth and Its Implications

The Internet is spreading rapidly the world over. In China, the Internet or *Hu-lian-wang* has been expanding at a breath-taking pace in recent years. Since its debut in 1994 with 1,600 registered users, China's Internet sector has experienced virtually exponential growth, with registered users increasing to 620,000 in 1997 and further to 2.1 million in 1998, the time when the Internet became globally popular. Even more spectacularly, as shown previously in Chart 4, the number of users in China in 1999 alone quadrupled to 8.9 million, compared to 4.5 million in Taiwan and 22 million in Japan.[29] By mid-2000, the number of Internet users in China, who were connected to cyberspace via 6.5 million or so computers, jumped to 16.9 million.[30] It was earlier estimated that by the end of 2000, the number of registered Internet users in China would swell to more than 20 million.[31] It now appears that the growth rate of the Internet in China has been somewhat underestimated.

---

[29]"Zoujin Hulianwang Shidai", *China Comment: Ban Yue Tan* (May 2000); "Japan reaches 22 million Internet users", *Asia Pacific Research Group* (16 March 2000), http://www.aprg.com/.html; and "55% of Net users in Taiwan have multiple accesses to the Internet", *Taiwan Chapter of the Internet Society* (31 January 2000), http://www.isoc.org.tw.

[30]Zhongguo Hulian Wangluo Fazhan Zhuang Kuang Tongji, *Zhongguo Hulian Wangluo Xinxi Zhongxin* (Beijing, July 2000), http://www.cnnic.net.cn.

[31]"2000 Nian Zhongguo IT Shida Yu Ce", *Xinhua Tongxun She* (28 January 2000), http://www.xinhua.org.

The number of websites in China has also increased sharply within a short span of time, from 3,700 in mid-1998 to 27,289 in mid-2000; whilst domain addresses, from 9,415 to over 99,743.[32] (Tables 2A and 2B list major Chinese government and popular Chinese websites, respectively. Table 2C lists the websites of various provinces and cities.) Currently, the international bandwidth for the networks is 1,234M.[33] By 2001, China aims at linking 80% of its local governments to the Internet and getting 80% of its large and medium companies wired.[34] Due to the widespread sharing of Internet accounts, the actual number of users in China is difficult to estimate; but the actual online population is certainly much larger than the registered number. By 2005, China could have 6.6% or some 85 million of its population online.[35]

The economic and social significance of the Internet is apparent from the profile of users. According to a survey conducted by the China's Internet Network Information Centre (CNNIC) in mid-2000, among the 16.9 million Internet users, 2.6 million used special lines, 11.8 used dial-up connections and 2.6 million used both means for Internet access.[36] In addition, 590,000 users made use of other appliances, such as mobile phones and home information technology appliances to establish Internet connections.

---

[32]Zhongguo Hulian Wangluo Fazhan Zhuang Kuang Tongji, *Zhongguo Hulian Wangluo Xinxi Zhongxin* (Beijing, July 2000), http://www.cnnic.net.cn and "Grim Forecast For Bulk of Cash-strapped Online Firms", *South China Morning Post* (23 June 2000).

[33]Zhongguo Hulian Wangluo Fazhan Zhuang Kuang Tongji, *Zhongguo Hulian Wangluo Xinxi Zhongxin* (Beijing, July 2000), http://www.cnnic.net.cn.

[34]"Surf's Up", *Far Eastern Economic Review* (4 March 1999).

[35]"Start-up aims for traditional firms", *South China Morning Post* (26 May 2000).

[36]Zhongguo Hulian Wangluo Fazhan Zhuang Kuang Tongji, *Zhongguo Hulian Wangluo Xinxi Zhongxin* (Beijing, July 2000), http://www.cnnic.net.cn.

Table 2A. List of Major Chinese Government Websites

MINISTRIES/DEPARTMENTS	WEBSITE ADDRESSES
Ministry of Public Security	http://gab.mps.gov.cn
Ministry of Education	http://www.mpe.edu.cn
Ministry of Civil Affairs	http://www.mca.gov.cn
Ministry of Finance	http://www.mof.gov.cn
Ministry of Construction	http://www.cin.gov.cn
Ministry of Railways	http://www.chinamor.cn.net
Ministry of Communications	http://www.moc.gov.cn
Ministry of Agriculture	http://www.agri.gov.cn
Ministry of Health	http://www.moh.gov.cn
Ministry of Information Industry	http://www.mii.gov.cn
Ministry of Foreign Affairs	http://www.fmprc.gov.cn
Ministry of Labour and Social Security	http://www.molss.gov.cn
Ministry of Land and Natural Resources	http://www.mlr.gov.cn
Ministry of Science and Technology	http://www.most.gov.cn
Ministry of Water Resources	http://www.mwr.gov.cn
Ministry of Culture	http://www.ccnt.gov.cn
Ministry of Foreign Trade and Economic Cooperation	http://www.moftec.gov.cn
State Economic and Trade Commission	http://www.setc.gov.cn
State Development Planning Commission	http://www.sdpc.gov.cn
State Family Planning Commission	http://www.sfpc.gov.cn

Source: "Zoujin Hulianwang Shidai", *China comment: Ban Yue Tan* (May 2000) and "New Structure of the State Council", *http://www.lib.umich.edu/libhome* (May 2000).

Table 2B. List of Top Ten Chinese Popular Websites

NAME OF WEBSITES	WEBSITE ADDRESSES
Sina.com	http://www.sina.com.cn
Sohu.com	http://www.sohu.com
Netease.com	http://www.163.com
Capital Online	http://www.263.net
Yahoo	http://cn.yahoo.com
163.net	http://www.163.net
21cn.com	http://www.21cn.com
Chinadotcom	http://www.china.com
ChinaRen	http://www.chinaren.com
Yesky Tianji Wang	http://www.yesky.com

Source: Zhongguo Hulian Wangluo Fazhan Zhuang Kuang Tongji, *Zhongguo Hulian Wangluo Xinxi Zhongxin* (Beijing, July 2000), http://www.cnnic.net.cn.

Table 2C. List of Websites of Various Regions/Provinces/Cities

REGIONS/PROVINCES/CITIES	WEBSITE ADDRESSES
Anhui	Http://www.ah.cninfo.net
Beijing	http://www.beijingscene.com
Chongqing	http://www.China-window.com/Chongqing
Fujian	http://www.fj.cninfo.net
Gansu	http://www.gs.cninfo.net
Guangdong	http://www.gd.cninfo.net
Guangxi	http://www.gx.cninfo.net
Guizhou	http://www.gz.cninfo.net
Hainan	http://www.hq.cninfo.net
Hebei	http://www.hebei-info.com
Heilongjiang	http://www.hl.cninfo.net
Henan	http://www.online.ha.cn
Hubei	http://www.hb.cninfo.net
Hunan	http://www.hn.cninfo.net
Inner Mongolia	http://www.nm.cninfo.net
Jilin	http://www.jl.cninfo.net
Jiangsu	http://www.js.cninfo.net
Jiangxi	http://www.jx.cninfo.net
Liaoning	http://www.China-liaoning.com
Qinghai	http://www.qh.cninfo.net
Shandong	http://www.sd.cninfo.net
Shanghai	http://www.online.sh.cn
Sichuan	http://www.sc.cninfo.net
Tianjin	http://www.tianjin-window.com
Tibet	http://www.Chinatibet.org
Yunnan	http://www.yn.cninfo.net
Zhejiang	http://www.zhejiangchina.com

Source: "Useful Links: Chinese Regions and Cities", *Chinaonline* (7 April 2000), http://www.chinaonline.com.

The survey also reported that 84% of Chinese Internet users (i.e. 14.2 million people) have college education and above; whilst 64% (10.8 million) are earning an average monthly income of more than 1,000 yuan.[37] As can be expected, most Internet users in China are young people: 86% of users (14.5 million) are between 18 and 35 years old. However, the percentage of male users, at 75% (12.7 million), is significantly higher than that of female users.[38] Most of the Internet users are single (67%) and they access the Internet mainly from home (59%), with most (56%) spending between 6 to 20 hours online per week. (See Charts 5, 6 and 7.)

In terms of usage, 56% of the online population used the Internet for gathering information while only 11%, 10% and 7% for education, entertainment and work purposes, respectively.[39] Most (70%) of the Internet users are interested in surfing for local news, with only a small number (10%) going for foreign news and information. Other reasons for going online include use of email, access to search engines, downloading software, chatting online, playing games as well as shopping online. Although over 70% surveyed have frequented e-commerce websites, only less than 20% and 8% have shopped and auctioned online, respectively.[40]

In China, as in other countries, young people are generally more computer-savvy. Currently, 67% of Chinese children in the big cities can use computers, with 17% of them knowing how to log on to the Internet. Of children who surf the Internet, 43% log on for information, and 48% visit chatrooms.[41] In the next five years, therefore, young people will constitute the largest proportion of home Internet users, with the average age of Internet users falling

---

[37] *Ibid.*
[38] *Ibid.*
[39] *Ibid.*
[40] *Ibid.*
[41] "Children Surfing into the Cyber-age", *China Daily* (2 June 2000).

Chart 5. Occupations/Industries of Internet Users in China (July 2000)

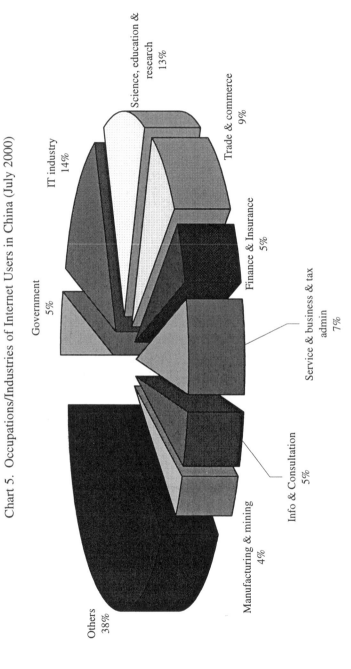

Science, education & research 13%

Trade & commerce 9%

IT industry 14%

Finance & Insurance 5%

Government 5%

Service & business & tax admin 7%

Info & Consultation 5%

Manufacturing & mining 4%

Others 38%

Source: Zhongguo Hulian Wangluo Fazhan Zhuang Kuang Tongji, *Zhongguo Hulian Wangluo Xinxi Zhongxin* (Beijing, July 2000), http://www.cnnic.net.cn.

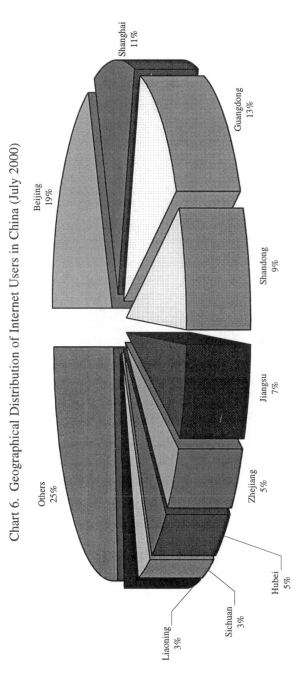

Chart 6. Geographical Distribution of Internet Users in China (July 2000)

Source: Zhongguo Hulian Wangluo Fazhan Zhuang Kuang Tongji, *Zhongguo Hulian Wangluo Xinxi Zhongxin* (Beijing, July 2000), http://www.cnnic.net.cn.

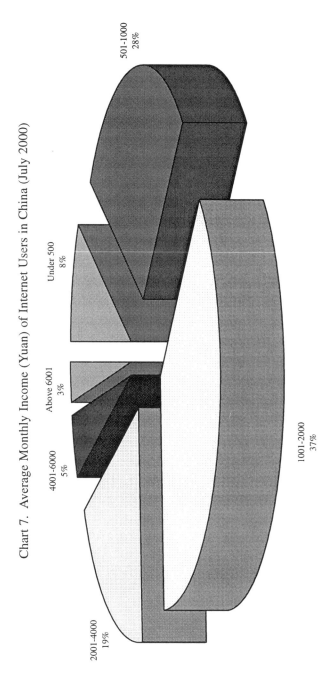

Chart 7. Average Monthly Income (Yuan) of Internet Users in China (July 2000)

Source: Zhongguo Hulian Wangluo Fazhan Zhuang Kuang Tongji, *Zhongguo Hulian Wangluo Xinxi Zhongxin* (Beijing, July 2000), http://www.cnnic.net.cn.

below 26 years old.[42] Furthermore, as the Internet continues to spread, the "net population" is likely to become less elitist, with more less-educated and lower-income groups becoming new Internet users.

Why has the Internet in China grown so rapidly in the short span of just a few years? First, the rapid growth is closely linked to the equally rapid development of the information technology (IT) infrastructure. In 1999, China had the world's second largest telephone network after the United States, with 110 million fixed telephone subscribers, in addition to 43 million mobile phones.[43] In 1999, the sales of PCs (personal computers) in China amounted to 4.9 million units, even though only about 3.5 million PCs were reported to have been directly wired to the net.[44] As in Japan, many Chinese users can soon skip the PC connectivity by jumping direct to the WAP (wireless application protocol) services. According to a recent survey on WAP, 30% of the mobile phone owners in China will potentially be mobile WAP users.[45] In fact, China Mobile Communications Corp., China's largest mobile network operator, expects the number of WAP-based consumers to hit 4 million in 2001.[46]

Secondly, contrary to outside impression, the Chinese government does not discourage the use of the Internet; instead it has been actually promoting it. Beijing takes the view that Internet

---

[42]"Appealing to Tomorrow's Internet Users", *China Business* (10 April 2000).

[43]"Home Phone Makers Gird for Fight", *China Business Weekly* (28 May–3 June 2000).

[44]Zhongguo Hulian Wangluo Fazhan Zhuang Kuang Tongji, *Zhongguo Hulian Wangluo Xinxi Zhongxin* (Beijing, January 2000), http://www.cnnic.net.cn.

[45]"WAP — Mobile Internet", *Xinhua News Agency,* http://www.xinhua.org/ssjj/wap/files.

[46]"China Mobile Targets Internet", *Eastwallstreet.com* (4 July 2000), http://international.yestock.com/english.

development can boost competitiveness and generate good economic returns.[47] In fact, China has planned a campaign to bring industries, government offices and households online as part of a strategy to make the Internet a powerful engine for economic growth.[48] President Jiang Zemin recently stated that "all young people, both Chinese and foreign, and all scientists and scholars around the world will make the best use of Internet".[49]

More specifically, apart from building up the basic Internet infrastructure, the government has taken direct measures to expand the bandwidth to keep up with rising demand, and to tighten Internet security from hackers. Above all, it has launched several "Golden Projects" to spearhead the IT growth and to promote IT applications. For instance, the Golden Bridge project is aimed at wiring millions of Chinese citizens to the nation-wide financial network by 2010. The Golden Card smart cards will facilitate financial transactions and payments with government departments.

Compared with the developed countries, China's Internet sector is admittedly technologically backward. It is also highly disintegrated, geographically concentrated in several large cities such as Beijing, Shanghai and Guangzhou; and involving mainly the younger and the more educated middle class. But the sheer number of Internet users has enabled China to reach a critical mass to jump-start the growth of its "new economy", even though many segments of its "old economy" remain backward. After its accession to the WTO, China can also count on foreign technology and foreign venture capital to spur further Internet development.

---

[47]Major services provided by Internet include electronic mail service (e-mail), document transmission (document download) service, world-wide-web (www) browsing service, electronic commerce and remote login service.

[48]"Wu Sees Internet As Growth Engine", *Hong Kong Standard* (30 March 2000).

[49]"Many Chinese Students Don't Go Back Home", *The Straits Times* (19 June 2000).

Indeed, China's potential as a leading Internet market in the world is well recognized by many foreign multinationals, many which are vying for a share of this growing market. Some even take the view that over the long run the Chinese language Internet may one day become a viable medium of communication, next to the English language, on account of a potentially large number of Chinese Internet users worldwide.[50] This could offset the short-term risks that foreign firms may have to bear by entering the Chinese market now. At present, Yahoo! and HongKong.com have already become large players in Greater China. Recently, Lycos in partnership with SingTel, has opened portal sites aimed at the same market.[51]

In the meanwhile, as the Internet grows and spreads, the Chinese government has already come face to face with the potential downside risks of the information society. In one of Beijing's clearest statements yet of its ambivalent attitude towards the Internet, the *People's Daily* recently acknowledged that while the Internet had extended the government's reach, rendering "political thought work" more efficient, it had also "become an important thought and public opinion battle front and a new realm for the struggle of international opinion.... Enemy forces at home and abroad are sparing no effort to use this battle front to infiltrate us".[52] As admitted by President Jiang Zemin, "the Internet has become a key battlefield in China's political and ideological struggle" and "foreign enemy forces are trying all they can with the Internet to win over the Chinese

---

[50]"Surfing the Web Chinese Style", *Asia 21* (September 1999).
[51]"Lycos Asia Opens Greater China Internet Portal Sites", *Hong Kong Standard* (23 May 2000).
[52]"Internet Brings Unwelcome Ideas", *South China Morning Post* (10 August 2000).

people".[53] Jiang therefore cautioned the Chinese people against the "possible distortion of facts" in the foreign net.

Nonetheless, despite its penchant for information control, Beijing has increasingly come to realize that the Internet can maintain only an informational boundary but not an effective wall between China and the world.[54] It is well known that the outlawed Falun Gong sect had used the Internet to communicate among its members — and the Chinese security apparatus had also made use of Internet to track them down! The Internet had also embarrassed Beijing by quickly spreading the high-level corruption scandal in Fujian. On 20 May 2000, many people on the Mainland had managed to beat the government's news blackout on Taiwan's newly elected President Chen Shui-bian's inaugural address by turning direct to the Internet. In fact, the Chinese authorities have set up the "net police" to routinely monitor certain politically oriented online chatrooms, e.g., portals carrying sensitive messages of the "June 4 movement".[55]

The government may still be ambivalent towards the new information society, but the Internet is starting to change the way young Chinese living in the large cities interact with each other, albeit slowly and subtly. Traditional industries, such as contemporary Chinese art, have been posted on virtual galleries in cyberspace. In chatrooms over the Internet, young people exchange views on everything ranging from sports to movie stars to current affairs, such as cross-straits relations with Taiwan. Many are able to read books from the online library, a project launched by the National Library in Beijing.

---

[53]"War on Net Hots Up", *South China Morning Post* (12 July 2000).

[54]See Mueller, M. and Tan, Zixiang (1997), *China in the Information Age*, US: Praeger Publishers.

[55]"Cyber-crackdown Fails To Silence Protesters", *South China Morning Post* (2 June 2000).

Foreigners are also able to learn about China and its culture through the Internet. When the Internet was first introduced in China, many Chinese depended on foreign websites for information. However, recent years have marked a rapid increase in the number of Chinese websites and there is an obvious reverse trend with more foreigners hitting Chinese domestic websites. Provincial and city officials are increasingly using websites to attract foreign investors by posting their localities' preferential investment policies and listing their state-owned enterprises that were up for sale. Chinese businesses are encouraged to post their product information online. Many Chinese websites also operate for online shopping. (The next chapter will discuss e-commerce in detail.)

In ushering in the new information society, the Internet is a boon to China's economic and social progress, yet it is also a bane to Beijing by posing a direct challenge to the Communist rule. The Party has yet to come to grips with the triple threat of an Internet society involving openness, transparency and democracy. Like other societies, China will also have to face the social problem of the so-called "digital divide", i.e., a small group of info-haves versus a large group of info-have-nots. It may be stressed that in China's vast countryside, many of the 900 million rural dwellers have never used a computer or even heard of the Internet.[56] China is presently plagued by growing income disparities among its different geographical regions and among its social classes. The Internet is going to aggravate this problem.

The Internet's Developments in China

In 1987, the China Academic Network (CANET) was established to support research and education activities in computer science. In

---

[56]"China's Uneven Advances", *International Herald Tribune* (17 March 1999).

1988, China made the first foray into the Internet age when CANET began to exchange e-mails with the global Internet indirectly via a link in Germany.[57] Among the early important networks in China were the Institute of High Energy Physics (IHEP), the Networking and Computing Facility of China (NCFC), the China Research Network (CRNET), and the Chinese Academy of Sciences Network (CASNET)[58] (See Box 1).

The academic networks, IHEP, NCFC, CRNET and CASNET, were subsequently consolidated into two major national systems: (1) the China Science and Technology Network (CSTNET), which was a product of interconnection involving 20 academic networks under the Chinese Academy of Sciences (CAS); and (2) the China Education and Research Network (CERNET), which was started by the State Education Commission for international links as well as for China's education, research and economic development.

In April 1994, China formally entered the Internet age when CAS's Computer Network Information Centre (CNIC) set up its first link-up with more than 30 research institutes through fibre optic cables. In the same year, the Ministry of Post and Telecommunications (MPT), which had wanted to be a carrier of China's networks and regulator-cum-administrator of China's Internet, constructed China's largest commercial network, the CHINANET. This was launched by China Telecom and aimed at providing various Internet services to public users and to promote the commercialization of the information network. The CHINANET includes 8 regional network centres that cover 31 provinces and cities. In 1996, Jitong, a company under the Ministry of Electronic

---

[57]Mueller, M. and Tan, Zixiang (1997), *China in the Information Age*, US: Praeger Publishers.
[58]Pecht, M., Lee, C. S., Zong, X. F., Jiang, J. L. and Wang, Y. W. (1999), *The Chinese Electronics Industry*, Washington, D. C.: CRC Press.

Box 1 Early Networks

NCFC — Networking and Computing Facility of China	NCFC, jointly established in 1989 by the State Planning Commission and the World Bank's Key Scientific Development Project, aimed to construct networks for technical scientific institutions in China. NFCF was made up of 4 parts, namely, Wide Area Network (WAN), Urban Area Network (main network), Campus Network and Local Area Network (LAN).
CRNET — China Research Network	CRNET, which was set up in 1990, used a link via Europe to exchange information with global networks.
CASNET — Chinese Academy of Sciences Network	The CASNET is divided into 2 parts: the branch campus network (established in 1992); and the application of long distance channels to connect all branch schools and research institutes to the NCFC network center's WAN. In 1995, CASNET connected the 12 branch campuses and various WAN.

Industry (MEI), developed the China Golden Bridge Network (CHINAGBN) with a large number of data networks.[59]

With the rapid growth of the Internet in China, the China Internet Network Information Centre (CNNIC), a non-profit organization, was established in June 1997 to perform the role of National Internet Network Information Centre for China. CNNIC also connects with the International Network Information Centre (InterNIC) and the

---

[59]By early 1996, several networks began to provide commercial services, charging connection and usage fees from users. A secondary market for Internet accounts was also developed and many users were reselling their accounts.

Asia & Pacific Ocean Internet Network Information Centre (APNIC). The main functions of the CNNIC include:

- To provide domain names registration service, Internet protocol addresses distribution and autonomous system codes (AS codes for short) distribution;
- To establish a national catalogues database;
- To provide information regarding network consumers, addresses, domain names, AS codes, and policies and regulations of Internet network in China;
- To collect statistics concerning the development of Internet in China;
- To provide training on Internet technology and application;
- To conduct research related to Internet; and
- To provide technical consultation services.

China's early networks were subsequently consolidated into six major networks — two public networks and four commercial ones — to form China's main Internet Service Providers (ISPs). Together, they constitute the backbone of China's Internet, accounting for roughly 80% of all Internet businesses. Operated under the supervision of the Ministry of Information Industry (MII), they are responsible for the bulk of network exchanges, transmissions and connections (See Box 2). Box 3 summarizes China's Internet development in chronological order.

Regulatory Framework

As the Internet becomes more widespread, the Chinese government is keenly aware of the implications of maintaining monopoly over the industry. Government monopoly provides a means of control, which will ensure that the Internet does not turn into a socially destabilizing force.

While the government is still struggling with the problem of how to set up an appropriate regulatory system to govern the fast-growing industry, the Chinese courts are already faced with an increasing number of cases involving disputes over the Internet, such as copyright infringements, plagiarism of homepages, publishing of information without authorization and hacking of websites.[60] Web-related cases appear to be difficult to deal with because there are no concrete statutes on Internet uses.[61] The lack of clear-cut laws concerning the Internet has led to a chaotic situation which leaves plaintiffs, defendants and judges bewildered.[62] Problems include not just jurisdictions but also the verification and definition of damages, and the validity of digitized evidence. To deliver justified rulings on Internet-related lawsuits, the Chinese legal community not only requires legal expertise but also industry knowledge. This presents a formidable challenge for the Chinese courts.

Although a formal set of rules and regulations governing the Internet industry has yet to take roots, the government has come up with several guidelines to regulate the industry (See Annexes 1, 2, 3, 4, 5 and 6):

- On 1 February 1996, the *PRC Interim Provisions on the Regulation of Computer Networks and the Internet* came into force to ensure the "healthy development of China's Internet" as well as strengthen the development of China's domain name system.

---

[60]Currently, more than 40% of Chinese websites have been hacked and 44% of them had their online information tampered with. See "40% of Websites Come Under Hacker Attack", *Hong Kong Standard* (5 April 2000).

[61]"Wu Sees Internet As Growth Engine", *Hong Kong Standard* (30 March 2000).

[62]"Internet-related Cases Challenge China's Courts", *China Daily* (27 March 2000).

Box 2 Current Major Networks in China

Public Networks	
China Education and Research Network (CERNET)	CERNET (http://www.cernet.edu.cn) is the network of China's Ministry of Education, linking China's major education and research institutes. CERNET consists of three levels of networks: the national backbone network, local networks and campus networks. Linking over 300 universities and colleges, CERNET provides mainly scientific research and educational information. The speed of CERNET's backbone network and its outlets were 512k bits/s and 2m bits/s, respectively.
Chinese Science and Technology Network (CSTNET)	CSTNET (http://www.csnet.net.cn) was established by the central government with loans from the World Bank. The Network Operation Centre under the CAS is in charge of its operation and management. CSTNET is made up of two major parts, the NCFC and the internal network of the CASNET. CSTNET has extended to all the major cities in China. Currently, its major users include 123 research institutions in the CAS system and more than 200 affiliated organizations. Although CSTNET offers its services to the public, the majority of its users are provincial- and local-government agencies and state-owned enterprises. Even though some of these enterprises have Internet access, CSTNET is primarily not a business-related network.
Commercial Networks	
China Public Computer Network (CHINANET)	CHINANET (http://www.chinanet.cn.net) was started in 1994 by the Ministry of Post and Telecommunications (MPT). China Telecom has been in charge of its construction, operation and management. Its network access number is 163. CHINANET's network structure is divided into three parts: the national backbone network, local-access networks and the national Network Operation Centre and Network Information Centre (NOC & NIC).

Box 2 (Continued)

	CHINANET has become China's dominant Internet provider, offering services in all major cities in China. As at end 1999, CHINANET had total bandwidth of 291Mbps of Chinese connections to the global Internet backbone. Though China Telecom itself is the dominant ISP for CHINANET, a few small ISPs operate by leasing CHINANET resources from China Telecom. But China Telecom's high leasing fees have effectively prevented these small ISPs from becoming significant players in the ISP business.
China Golden Bridge Network (CHINAGBN)	CHINAGBN (http://www.gb.com.cn) is operated by Jitong Communication Co. Ltd. Its network access number is 167. In January 1994, the state-owned Jitong was founded to operate the network, but did not launch its CHINAGBN services until September 1996 (9 months after CHINANET). Jitong is also the main ISP for CHINAGBN, offering IP telephony and other Internet services. The major objectives of the CHINAGBN are to establish a public economic information network, to interconnect the heterogeneous private network of multiple departments and sectors, and to establish a computer information system for government agencies and private enterprises.
China Unicom Public Computer Interconnection Network (UNINET)	UNINET (http://www.uninet.com.cn), which is run by China Unicom, China's second telephone operator, has developed extensive cellular and paging services. The UNINET's network access number is 165. In southern China, Unicom is using its IP network, UNINET, for IP applications such as Voice over IP and Fax on IP. It has plans to introduce comprehensively basic and value-added data communications services and offer Internet-access services on UNINET in 100 cities in 2000.

Box 2 (Continued)

China Network Communications Public Interconnection Network (CNCNET)	CNCNET was established by the CAS, the State Administration of Radio, Film and TV, the Ministry of Railways and some related organizations in Shanghai. CNCNET, in future, will be run by the new China Network Communications (China Netcom), which is still at its planning stages. China Netcom will offer wholesale broadband access as well as local Internet service in major Chinese cities. Its network access number is 171. CNCNET will be connected to existing broadcasting and railway networks.

Box 3 China's Internet Development Timeline

Time	Significant Events
Sep 1987	Qian Tianbai, a professor in Beijing, sent out the first e-mail in China through the Chinese Academic Network (CANET).
1988	ECNETM, hosted by the Institute of High Energy Physics (IHEP) in the Chinese Academy of Sciences (CAS), was able to exchange e-mails with Europe and North America.
Oct 1990	Represented by Prof. Qian Tianbai, China registered the country's domain name, cn, at DDN-NIC, the predecessor of InterNIC (a cooperative domain name registration service between the U.S. Government and Network Solutions, Inc.).
Jun 1992	The Chinese government and the U.S. National Science Foundation discussed the possibility of connecting China to the Internet. However, China was informed that China's access to the Internet would encounter political barriers due to the presence of U.S. government agencies on the Internet at that time.
Mar 1993	The specialized line that connected the IHEP to Stanford University started operation. The IHEP rented the line from AT&T's international satellite channel.
Aug 1993	Premier Li Peng approved US$3 million in funding for the construction of the Golden Bridge Network project, China's first national public economic information network.

Box 3 (Continued)

Time	Significant Events
Dec 1993	The National Economic Informationization Joint Conference was set up and Vice Premier Zhou Jiahua was appointed as the chairman.
Apr 1994	The NCFC project (aimed at building an information superhighway in Peking University, Tsinghua University and the Chinese Academy of Sciences) was connected via Sprint to the Internet.
May 1994	The IHEP in the Chinese Academy of Sciences set up the first web server and developed the first homepage in China. The CN first level domain name registration server was moved from Germany to China.
Sep 1994	China Telecom signed an agreement with U.S. Secretary of Commerce Ron Brown to start two specialized lines (in Beijing and Shanghai) through Sprint.
Jan 1995	The two specialized lines in Beijing and Shanghai came into operation, creating public access to the Internet. China's first online magazine started operation.
Jan 1996	A national informationization leadership group was set up under the State Council; Vice Premier Zhou Jiahua was appointed the chairman. China Public Computer Internet (CHINANET) started operation.
Mar 1996	The IETF (Internet Engineering Task Force) approved the first standards for Chinese character transmission.
Sep 1996	China Golden Bridge Network (CHINAGBN) started operation.
Dec 1996	The China Public Multimedia Network hosted by China Telecom opened, and the first batch of local websites including Shanghai Online was launched.
Jun 1997	The Chinese Academy of Sciences (CAS) set up the China Internet Network Information Center (CNNIC) to oversee China's Internet development.

Box 3 (Continued)

Time	Significant Events
Nov 1997	The first CNNIC Report on China's Internet was released, with biannual updates to follow. As of 31 Oct 1997, there were 299,000 computers in China connected to the Internet, 620,000 Internet subscribers, 4,066 .cn domain names, and 1,500 websites.
Mar 1998	The Ministry of Information Industry (MII) was established.
Jun 1998	The second CNNIC Report on China's Internet was released. There were over 542,000 computers accessing the Internet and some 1.2 million Internet subscribers, 9,451 .cn domain names and 3,700 websites.
Jan 1999	CNNIC released the third national survey, which claimed there were 747,000 computers in China connected to the Internet, 2.1 million Internet subscribers, 18,396 .cn domain names, and 5,300 websites.
Jun 1999	The fourth CNNIC Report on China's Internet was released. The survey showed 1.46 million computers connected to the Internet in China, 4 million Internet subscribers, 29,045 .cn domain names and 9,906 websites.
Jan 2000	The fifth CNNIC Report on China's Internet was released, showing 3.5 million computers connected to the Internet in China, 9 million Internet subscribers, 48,695 .cn domain names and 15,153 websites. At the same time, a special computer network, http://www.5000.gov.cn, started a trial run to connect the Chinese government's economic departments with 5,000 of the country's large enterprises which uses the Internet to send their operational information and statistics directly to the State Statistical Bureau.[63] The enterprises also provide detailed information such as annual statistics, quarterly investment in basic construction, technological upgrade, R&D (research and development) and payroll, monthly output, sales, sales revenues, profits, orders and inventory of key products. The network includes 60–70% of China's industries and covers over 2,000 products made by these enterprises.

[63]"China Data Network Provides 5,000 Companies' Results Directly to Ministry", *China Information* (27 January 2000).

Box 3 (Continued)

Time	Significant Events
Mar 2000	Chinese network operators such as China Telecom, China Unicom, China Netcom and China Jitong announced that they would inject US$1 billion into developing the Internet infrastructure in the same year,[64] signalling increased competition in the sector and potentially lucrative contracts for foreign equipment suppliers. The heavy spending is expected to boost creaky infrastructure via expanding digital networks, establishing or developing the asynchronous transfer mode (ATM)[65] and Internet Protocol (IP), expanding the capacity of the backbone and spurring sluggish web speeds.
Jul 2000	The sixth CNNIC Report on China's Internet was released, showing 6.5 million computers connected to the Internet in China, 16.9 million Internet subscribers, 99,734 .cn domain names and 27,289 websites. Over 40 famous Internet enterprises and news media websites amalgamated to form China's first academic Internet research organization — the National Internet Society.[66] The sponsors of the National Internet Society include state media websites such as the People's Daily Internet Edition, Xinhua Net and China Central Television; noted e-commerce websites such as Sina.com, NetEase.com, Sohu.com and 8848.net; as well as ISPs such as the A-1 Net and 263.net. Such an establishment suggests a trend toward joint development in the Chinese Internet industry. The National Internet Society is part of the Chinese Society of Information Economy. After its establishment, the former will invite a group of Internet scholars and consultants to provide consultancy services to Internet companies, as well as hold symposiums. Moreover, the Society will offer opportunities for international exchange and short-term professional training.

---

[64]"China To Spend US$1 billion on Internet Backbone", *South China Morning Post* (8 March 2000).

[65]The ATM is a high-speed technology which blends data, voice, and video in a single pipe.

[66]"Over 40 Websites Unite to Form Internet Society", *Mingpao* (29 July 2000).

- In April 1996, the *PRC Measures On The Regulation of Public Computer Networks And The Internet* were issued by the Ministry of Post and Telecommunications.
- In December 1997, the *Computer Information Network and Internet Security, Protection and Management Regulations* were approved by the State Council for promulgation by the Ministry of Public Security.
- In January 2000, the Bureau for the Protection of State Secrets (State Secrets Bureau) issued the *State Secrecy Protection Regulations For Computer Information Systems On The Internet* to limit online content.
- In February 2000, the Shanghai Personnel Bureau and the Office of the Shanghai Municipal Leading Group for National Economy and Social Information Technology Development jointly issued the *Rules of Shanghai Municipality On The Management Of Computer Public Information Networks Involving Personnel Exchange Services* to standardize the activities and ensure legal rights and interests of personnel exchange services by means of computer public information networks.
- On 1 September 2000, the latest text of regulations for business websites issued by the Beijing Municipal Administration for Industry and Commerce took effect.

Under the new rules, all websites are required to go through security checks. According to the State Secrets Bureau, "all organisations and individuals are forbidden from releasing, discussing or transferring state secret information on bulletin boards, chatrooms, or via Internet news groups. Any website that provides or releases information on the world-wide-web must undergo security checks and approval". Failure to do so will result in the government re-organizing or closing down the website.

The new laws effectively ban any information which has not been officially released. Furthermore, companies using encryption software, which allows confidential information like credit card details to be sent via the net, must register it with the government. These are arguably the harshest laws to be found in cyberspace, which could adversely affect China's fast-growing IT industry.

In April 2000, the Internet Information Management Bureau (IIMB) was established under the State Council Information Office (SCIO) to regulate the Internet media and improve the websites of five well-known state media, namely, the China Daily, the People's Daily, Xinhua News Agency, China Radio International and SCIO's China Internet Information Centre (CCIC). The main functions of IIMB include:

- To speed up news reporting on the state media websites through the streamlining of the censorship process;
- To spice up the content on the state media websites;
- To guide the state media websites in their preparation for public listing — to finance their transformation and development;
- To establish copyright standards and protect the legal rights and interests of information providers;
- To standardize news dissemination;
- To stamp out false and harmful information that misleads readers;
- To eliminate pornography and online gambling;
- To supervise and ensure accuracy of information and news posted on Internet websites;
- To promote healthy and orderly development of all websites, online news coverage and related Internet services; and
- To guide Chinese ICPs in preparation for China's entry into the World Trade Organization (WTO).

Prior to the introduction of these measures, these traditional media had been greatly hindered by several layers of bureaucratic censorship which they had to undergo before their news could be released to the public, so much so that the news on the websites were often out-dated. Furthermore, their content was also unexciting.

Demand Side Issues

It may be remembered that while Internet access is growing at an unprecedented rate, it is still denied to millions of Chinese. In China today, although the number of subscribed Internet users is growing rapidly, it represents only a small fraction of China's 1.2 billion population, i.e., approximately 1% of its total population. Such a small base, coupled with a low PC penetration rate, points to a limited information pool in the Chinese language. This is largely due to the fact that the vast majority of Chinese still cannot afford a home computer.[67] Worse still, many computers are not networked together, thus further limiting the scope for users to gain access to the Internet. As the major information networks are in English, China's Internet will really take off only when users in future are able to surf in Chinese and tap into a large and useful pool of information and data in Chinese.

Furthermore, among China's 40 million or so enterprises, only 10% of their Chief Executive Officers understand what the Internet is really about.[68] The remaining 90% need to be educated that via the Internet, people all over the world are supposed to be connected as one and economic transactions become borderless, unrestricted by physical barriers. With rapid progress in Internet usage, Chinese enterprises would, therefore, need to quickly adapt to technological changes and establish online connections with global businesses in order to tap onto their benefits.

Other major obstacles include high charges for using Internet, slow transmission speed, and government control on information

---

[67]The average cost of a low-end, domestic-made personal computer is 6000 yuan. The price is relatively high compared to Chinese workers' income. See "Surf's Up For Cellphone Net Users", *Chinaonline* (7 July 2000).

[68]"Zhongguo liaojie hulianwang de qiye lauzong budao yicheng", *Zhongguo Jingji Xinxiwang* (14 July 2000).

access for security reasons. Most individuals who subscribe to the Internet have to pay fees in two parts: one to the ISP and another to the Chinese telecom operator for the use of the telephone line. Internet access fee is currently set at 4 yuan (US$0.48) per hour while fixed line telephone charge is 1.8 yuan (US$0.21) per hour, the same rate as the cost of local telephone calls.[69] This means that an individual has to fork out about 6 yuan per hour in order to surf the net, which is rather expensive, considering the relatively low average income in China. In fact, according to a survey conducted by CCNIC, 36% users complained of the high cost of using the Internet.[70] In addition, some 49% of Internet users feel that the connection or transmission speed to cyberspace is too slow.[71]

MII has allowed CHINANET, CHINAGBN, UNINET, and CNCNET to become business networks providing commercial connections. MII has also given approval to them for the trial use of Internet Protocol (IP) telephony.[72] However, the government still bans foreign investment in these four companies, and had in fact forced Unicom and its subsidiary UNINET to wind up its initial commercial arrangements with foreign investors under the so-called "China-China-Foreign" (C-C-F) deal.[73]

---

[69]"China Internet Access Fees Too High", *Chinaonline* (4 April 2000), http://www.chinaonline.com.

[70]China Internet Network Information Center, *Statistical Report of the Development of China Internet* (Beijing, July 2000), http://www.cnnic.net.cn.

[71]*Ibid.*

[72]Internet Protocol telephony is a service which transmits phone calls via standard phone lines or broadband.

[73]Under this model, foreign investors tried to break into the monopoly by investing in a joint venture with a Chinese company, which in turn is usually a joint venture between a foreign firm and a local company, and routing the funds through the joint venture into a network operator, e.g., Unicom. The foreign investor receives either a fixed return on invested funds or a percentage of network revenues.

Although China does not allow cable companies to offer telephony, some experiments with Internet services are under way. While the State Council, through the State Leading Group on Information Technology (chaired by Vice Premier Wu Bangguo), still bans cable networks from offering telecommunications services,[74] including IP telephony, local pilot projects in Qingdao, Guangzhou and Shenzhen have launched cable television networks offering experimental broadband Internet access. This means that cable TV subscribers who do not have a PC or prefer not to use one can still access the Internet after simple technical modifications to their TV sets. However, subscribers are not allowed to make phone calls via this service.

Network operators are the biggest buyers of Internet-related products such as IP telephony and cable modem. While central-government control over network planning and operations remains, regional agencies including state-owned enterprises are increasingly free to make their own purchasing decisions. In fact, central and provincial governments have earmarked more funds to get various government agencies and key state-owned enterprises to make more use of the Internet.

As can be expected, ISPs in China currently offer little information on sensitive political, economic and social matters. Besides imposing strict rules on the dissemination of undesirable information that is considered detrimental to social value or national security, the Chinese government also censors sites operated by some U.S. news agencies like CNN and human rights groups. An intranet, China Wide Web, has been created to filter such sensitive news.

---

[74]In October 1999, the directive, "Suggestions on the Reinforcement of the Administration of Wired Broadcast and Cable TV Network Construction", was issued by the General Office of the State Council to prohibit telecommunications and cable companies from encroaching on each other's businesses.

As mentioned earlier, China has set up a special "net police unit" to monitor overall Internet activity. The State Information Security Appraisal and Identification Management Committee, which was recently established to protect government and commercial confidential files on the Internet, reportedly can identify users and monitor information from unauthorized uses. It also operates inspection centres and laboratories to provide technical support.

Currently, only Internet access providers approved by MII are licensed to operate an Internet café (known as *Wangba* in Chinese). An Internet café must first register with the local public security bureau, which will run security checks on these cafés. In fact, no one will be allowed to operate an Internet café without licenses from three separate agencies, namely, the local public security bureau, the local industry and commerce administration bureau, and the local telecommunications bureau. Internet café operators are to ensure that users do not "endanger national security" or social stability.[75]

It was reported that Chinese police, in 1999, closed down more than 300 illegal cyber-cafes in Shanghai for offering Internet services without a license. In Fujian, 45 Internet cafés were closed for providing pornography or for providing unlicensed electronic games.[76] In fact, Internet game playing — a common social activity among the young Chinese men — accounts for almost 70% of business in the Internet cafés.[77]

Chinese users, who can tap into the Internet via certain servers, are supposed to have registered with the local police and sign an

---

[75]"Surf's Up", *Far Eastern Economic Review* (Hong Kong, 4 March 1999).

[76]"Police Net 300 Illegal Web Cafes", *South China Morning Post* (9 June 1999) and "Internet Cafes Closed", *South China Morning Post* (19 June 2000).

[77]"In China, the Web is All Play", *International Herald Tribune* (3 July 2000).

undertaking not to harm national interests. However, there are numerous loopholes and implementation gaps. Internet users are still able to gain access to restricted sites by dialing overseas access numbers or calling up unrestricted sites for indirect access to restricted ones. Some ISPs are known to provide dial-up services without requiring users to register their personal information.[78]

Against its control instinct, the government also wants to see the Chinese society adapting to the IT age in an orderly manner. There are signs that the Chinese government is shifting from how to control information dissemination to how information can be usefully exploited. Ultimately, the government intends to exploit the Internet for such new opportunities as promoting exports and expanding domestic e-commerce so long as domestic stability is not seriously compromised.

The Chinese government is obviously very ambivalent towards such a "new baby" of the IT age as the Internet. On the surface, the government is inclined to control the information inflow. In reality, the government has been quietly lifting curbs on Internet access by allowing users to access some Western news sites. In 1998, President Clinton was spotted in one of Shanghai's Internet cafés, personally witnessing how Chinese people had been exposed to Western ideas in cyberspace.[79] In July 2000, the U.S. Secretary of State, Madeleine Albright, during her visit to Beijing, also tested for herself in a

---

[78]Beijing Telecom, a subsidiary of China Telecom, started a popular service in December 1997, called Capital Online, whereby users just dial 2631 and input user name 263 to gain access to the Internet without any paperwork. In addition, another Beijing ISP, Homeway, also started a public multimedia network, the 169 network, to allow customers to gain access to Internet without paperwork. However, non-registered users can only access Internet sites within China.

[79]"Net Fears", *China In Focus: Spring Issue No. 8* (June 2000).

local Internet café on the actual degree of free access by Chinese websites.[80]

The Chinese government has in fact already released more useful information such as government policies and economic data once closely guarded by government departments. Currently, Chinese government departments have more than 2,400 websites, but many are not updated for the convenient use of the public. Furthermore, few Chinese government websites offer an interactive function by which the public can ask questions or offer their own opinions. Government departments are simply not interested in the views of the public. As the websites are not updated regularly, the latest information (usually laws and regulations, policies and statistics issued by various government departments) would not be available to the public, thus forfeiting the very purpose of setting up these websites.[81]

China's entry to the WTO will lead to greater liberalization of the IT industry, particularly for the telecom sector. This will in turn spur faster growth of the Internet due to greater foreign participation; but it will also complicate the government's control measures. The Chinese government has yet to establish a security authentication system to enhance the materials/content provided online, and to implement an effective legal framework compatible with international standards. There is therefore still a lot of uncertainty over the future development of China's Internet industry in the next few years.

Supply Side Issues

For ISPs, MII is the agency authorized to review, approve and grant operation licenses. In this sector, foreign ownership is not allowed

---

[80]"Ao Qingqin Shi Beijing Wangzhan Ziyoudu", *Mingpao* (4 July 2000).
[81]"Party Line Rules in Cyberspace", *South China Morning Post* (5 June 2000).

to exceed 50%.[82] In 1999, the Chinese government approved more than 300 ISPs.[83] Among them were 53 companies approved by MII for nationwide services, and more than 250 firms approved by provincial post and telecom authorities (PTAs) for province-wide services. Tight regulation and strict licensing of ISPs has hampered the development of China's Internet infrastructure. These ISPs act more like Internet re-sellers and many are usually government-owned or backed.

Although MII controls the approval of ISPs, it does not regulate the approval for ICPs, estimated to be more than 1,000 nationwide.[84] ICPs are regulated by the relevant government departments such as the SCIO, the State Administration of Radio, Film and Television and the Ministry of Culture. The State Council announced in February 2000 that ICPs in China would be subjected to new rules and regulations. Specifically, they must meet two requirements before publishing news online. First, they need to obtain approval from the pertinent branch of the SCIO. Second, the website must obtain an operating license from MII. The SCIO does not intend to regulate the ICP sector too tightly. It is instituting these rules or measures mainly for protecting intellectual property rights and for ensuring greater reliability of news and information on the net, as part of the government's efforts to step up the supervision and improvement of news online provided by ICPs.

Although most of the 300 ISPs are owned by non-MII affiliates, they are basically still state-controlled or semi-government in nature. The major ISP, CHINANET, which provides access for about 800,000 Internet users in China, is actually the Internet arm of

---

[82]"China to Oversee ICP, ISP Regulations Promised by Q1", *Chinaonline* (5 January 2000), http://www.chinaonline.com.
[83]"Zhongguo Dianxinye Jin Ru Duo Yuan Jingzheng Shidai," *Xinhua Tongxun She* (16 February 2000), http://www.xinhua.org/chanjing.
[84]*Ibid.*

China Telecom. The rest of the ISPs have to make do with the remaining Internet users for their respective subscriber bases. The government has stipulated that all ISPs must use China Telecom's national infrastructure, while all international Internet traffic must travel through the networks of government-owned enterprises — CERNET, CHINANET, CHINAGBN and CSTNET.

It may be noted that most ISPs are currently losing money, mainly caused by exorbitant charges for the leased lines by China Telecom. China's ISPs spend about 80% of their total budget on line rental as compared to 5–6% in America.[85] Although China has recently reduced telecom charges, many ISPs are still unable to make ends meet. Not surprisingly, 88% of the ISPs in Beijing were reported to be delinquents in paying up their bills![86] Lowering the lease line fees is expected to benefit consumers as well, provided that Chinese ISPs pass the savings to subscribers. The existing high cost of getting online has undoubtedly been a barrier to entry for a large number of Chinese users.

In fact, the rental rates for ISPs are positively related to the number of subscriber-traffic routed through the leased lines.[87] This means, rather pervasively, that ISPs actually lose more money as their users multiply! Hence, it is impossible for them to charge low prices and reinvest for network development or for service upgrading. A few ISPs have successfully lowered their costs by establishing special relationship with MII and China Telecom.[88]

---

[85]The Economic Intelligence Unit, *Business China* (28 September 1998).

[86]"Beijing ISPs Can't Pay Their Bills", *Chinaonline* (1 December 1999), http://www.chinaonline.com.

[87]In other words, the more subscriber traffic an ISP routes, the higher the rental rate.

[88]For instance, Canada InfoNet, working in partnership with China Telecom, paid only 5000 yuan for the installation of Internet lines, whilst Sparkice, without connections, paid over 300,000 yuan.

Besides the lack of effective financing and support for Internet companies domestically, the prevailing poor IPO market sentiment in the world will also affect ISPs which are seeking for a listing on Nasdaq.[89] In view of the difficult market that ISPs are now experiencing, the next few years would see a shake-up in the industry, with weaker ISPs being weeded out and stronger ISPs emerging. In fact, the industry is already entering a consolidation phase, with smaller players dying out and larger ones merging. For instance, Sina.com, a leading Chinese portal, merged with PC Home Online in late 1999; while Netease.com formed an alliance with counterparts in Taiwan and Hong Kong for more traffic and more advertising revenues.

In short, commercial Internet businesses in China, other than major state-owned ISPs, are facing major difficulties arising from slow network connections, high operating costs, an uncertain regulatory environment, and direct competition from the telecom operators who are currently dominating the market. These problems need to be effectively tackled before the next spurt of Internet growth.

Opportunities for Foreign Involvement

Some ISPs have taken in foreign participation under various guises, despite the government's manifest prohibition of foreign ownership or foreign management in ISP ventures. Foreign ventures, with

---

[89]However, China Unicom, which kicked off its IPO on 29 May 2000, aimed to raise HK$41 billion (US$5.26 billion) in a Hong Kong and New York dual listing. If the option is fully exercised and the issue is priced at the top of the range, its IPO will be the largest ever for an Asian company outside Japan. See "China Tech IPOs Face Jittery U.S.", *Washington Post* (29 May 2000) and "China Unicom prices huge IPO", *MSNBC* (30 May 2000).

their necessary technological backup, have been attracted to China because of its rapidly growing Internet businesses. These foreign companies have entered the Chinese market by channeling their investment into ISPs via joint ventures with Chinese companies or collaborating with state-owned ISPs.[90] In mid-1999, China allowed the first entry of a foreign investor into the ISP market.[91] This venture took the China-China-Foreign (C-C-F) format, which, as mentioned earlier, was subsequently suspended by MII.

Penetrating China's Internet-related markets, understandably, requires a lot of patience and a highly focused approach. If a firm approaches the market with a long-term view, then it may be a good strategic move to enter now. In contrast to the existing uncertain legal environment surrounding Internet-service and -content provision, high-end software and hardware products (especially for customized servers and equipment used in large systems) are permitted. But such products will need intensive after-sales service as well as technology support from their foreign representative offices or foreign-owned enterprises located in China.

For ICP-related investments, American investors have set the trend, particularly in their involvement with Chinese ICP portals. Sohu.com attracted Intel, Dow Jones & Co., International Data Group (IDG) and the Massachusetts Institute of Technology (MIT);

---

[90]In mid-1999, Cenpok InfoCom, whose shareholders include the subsidiaries of the MII, received approval from the central government to sell a 30% stake in the firm directly to foreign investors.

[91]US-based company, Hartcourt, acquired 90% of a joint venture, China Infohighway Communications (CIH), the mainland's third-largest ISP owned by the Chinese government and which has an exclusive licence to offer commercial ISP services to 100,000 subscribers. Hartcourt, which would inject $30 million into CIH to cover existing liabilities and provide working capital, will manage CIH through AsiaNet, its wholly owned subsidiary. See "US firm buys 90% of mainland ISP", *South China Morning Post* (30 March 1999).

while China Infohighway has formed an alliance with Microsoft. In addition, Sina.com and China.com have Dell Computer and America Online (AOL), respectively, as their backers. These investments and partnerships are only a few of the growing number of strategic alliances formed between local and American-based Internet businesses.

The gradual opening up of the service provider market to foreign investment would certainly benefit local service providers, who are badly in need of new capital injection to meet high costs. They also have problems in obtaining bank loans and in seeking a listing on the stock exchange. More foreign involvement in the future would eventually lead to an increase in network capacity, making expansion considerably cheaper. However, until China's regulatory environment becomes more transparent, foreign investment in Chinese ISPs remains risky.

Legal ambiguity governing foreign investment in Internet businesses increases risks. The government's ban on foreign investment in ISPs has been explicit, while, in practice, it is more flexible towards ICPs. The government's underlying motives in excluding foreign involvement are to protect national security and economic interests. But this will change once China is in WTO. In fact, the future legal framework for foreign involvement in China's Internet sector is likely to evolve under the umbrella of WTO rules. What remains unclear is the speed of such an evolution. China prefers a smooth and orderly process of market opening, based on a more effective regulatory regime such as licensing arrangements. Foreign companies eyeing the China's Internet market hence need to be realistic, even after China's accession to WTO.

E-COMMERCE IN CHINA

E-commerce Mushrooms Despite Problems

"Electronic Commerce" or "e-commerce" has spread to China. Known in Chinese as *Dianzi Shangwu,* e-commerce has been the main driving force behind the development of the Internet, which, as pointed out in Chapter 2, has experienced spectacular growth in China in recent years. The term "e-commerce" is often used interchangeably with other similar terms like "e-tailing", "e-business" and "I-commerce" (Internet commerce). E-commerce can be classified into business-to-business (B2B), business-to-consumer (B2C), consumer-to-consumer (C2C), business-to-business-to-consumer (B2B2C) and business-to-consumer-to-business (B2C2B). In China, e-commerce is officially defined as profit-making activities on the Internet by commercial dealers and organizations.[92]

In China, as in elsewhere, e-commerce as part of the emerging new economy and starting from a low base, has experienced an upsurge recently. In 1999, China's e-commerce websites reported a total revenue of 200 million yuan (US$24.1 million), or twice as

---

[92]As defined in the *Circular of the Beijing Municipal Administration for Industry and Commerce Concerning Commerce Activities Registration,* issued by the Beijing Municipal Administration for Industry and Commerce on 28 March 2000.

much as in 1998.[93] For B2C e-commerce, or online shopping alone, the total turnover in 1999 amounted to 55 million yuan.[94] China's online sales is expected to triple in 2000 to 224.1 million yuan, and further to 40 billion yuan by 2004.[95] However, these e-commerce figures do not fully reflect the true amount of all e-commerce transactions. Many "e-commerce" transactions in China typically involve selecting a product online but paying offline, usually via cash-on-delivery, much like the pizza delivery in America.[96] As such, China's actual e-commerce revenue is more than double the formal "online shopping figures", which is expected to reach 10 billion yuan by the year 2002. It would be difficult for official statistics to fully capture the size of the entire sector, especially the "quasi-e-commerce" segment.

In absolute terms, the size of e-commerce in China today is still very small, accounting for only 0.018% of its total retail sales, as compared to the US$33 billion turnover or 1.4% of total retail sales in the United States.[97] Besides the "offline purchase online payment" practice mentioned earlier, another reason for the small figure is because credit cards have only recently become relatively widespread in urban China, and not many credit card holders feel comfortable

---

[93]"MII Puts Out Its Own 1999 E-commerce Figures", *Chinaonline* (20 January 2000), http://www.chinaonline.com.

[94]"Beijing Website Serves Elderly Shoppers", *China Daily Business Weekly* (2–8 July 2000).

[95]"Demand for Internet Sales Ready to Soar", *South China Morning Post* (6 September 2000).

[96]"MII Puts Out Its Own 1999 E-commerce Figures", *Chinaonline* (20 January 2000), http://www.chinaonline.com.

[97]"E-commerce in China: The CCIDnet Survey", *CCIDnet.com* (27 April 2000). CCIDnet.com is the website of the Center of Computer and Microelectronics Industry Development, which is the research and development arm of the Ministry of Information Industry (MII). http://www.ccidnet.com.

enough in using them online.[98] In fact, only 14% of China's 16.9 million or so Internet users are reported to have tried online shopping (including purchasing a product online, online auctions, online distance learning such as correspondence courses, etc.), compared to about 40% internationally.[99]

Furthermore, only 47.2% of these e-shoppers were satisfied with the goods and services.[100] While 45.5% of Internet users chose to shop online because of the time saved compared to conducting traditional commerce, 39.5% shopped online due to curiosity.[101] As to be expected, most e-shoppers are primarily young middle-class males with better education and higher incomes (China's yuppies), and mainly from Shanghai, Beijing and Guangdong.

According to another survey conducted by the China Internet Network Information Centre (CNNIC) in mid-2000, when asked about the reasons they held back from using e-commerce, 46% of Internet users said that they felt insecure to conduct online

---

[98]Indeed, credit cards have become quite widespread today, with over 50 million credit cards issued in 1999. Those with over 10,000 yuan in their bank accounts can apply for a credit card. As personal savings in China are high, many people own a credit card. Currently, MasterCard has 35 million holders in China. About 30%, 31% and 25% of the population in Beijing, Shanghai and Guangzhou owns credit cards, respectively. See "Status Quo and Development of China's E-commerce", *China Economic Information Network* (5 August 1999), http://www.cei.gov.cn/sicnet; "MasterCard to lead consumer revolution", *China Daily* (5 July 2000); and The Economic Intelligence Unit: What Chinese urbanites are buying, *Business China* (3 July 2000).

[99]Zhongguo Hulian Wangluo Fazhan Zhuang Kuang Tongji, *Zhongguo Hulian Wangluo Xinxi Zhongxin* (Beijing, July 2000), http://www.cnnic.net.cn; and "E-commerce In China: The CCIDnet Survey", *CCIDnet.com,* (27 April 2000), http://www.ccidnet.com.

[100]Zhongguo Hulian Wangluo Fazhan Zhuang Kuang Tongji, *Zhongguo Hulian Wangluo Xinxi Zhongxin* (Beijing, July 2000), http://www.cnnic.net.cn.

[101]*Ibid.*

transactions, 17% doubted the information posted over the Internet, 12% feared that after-sales services might not be provided and 10% feared that goods and services ordered online might not be delivered on time.[102]

Nonetheless, e-commerce and its related technologies have made a successful debut in urban China, hitting such sectors of the economy as retail and wholesale trade, securities and banking, travel, pharmaceutical, construction, shipping and foreign trade. Broadly speaking, the major participants of e-commerce in China in 1999 included the 40 million or so who had registered with the China Securities Transaction Net, those who bought 55 million airline tickets through electronic booking systems, and an unknown number of those who used the net for cargoes and freight in international trade.[103]

With comparatively low costs and simplified trading procedures, online enterprises, especially those dealing with e-business, have drawn increasing attention and evolved web business into an economic revolution. The emergence of B2B, B2B2C and B2C2B websites was a response to this trend.

At the B2C level, efficient online shopping networks provide many creative ways for the country's well-to-do urban consumers to spend more of their disposable income, thereby boosting domestic demand. At the B2B level, an international e-commerce framework could create a life-line to ailing state-owned firms, minimising much of the time-wasting and structural weaknesses from which the current system suffers.[104]

---

[102]*Ibid.*

[103]"Status Quo and Development of China's E-commerce", *China Economic Information Network* (5 August 1999). http://www.cei.gov.cn/sicnet.

[104]"Pay day, at last", *Business China* (17 July 2000).

To keep track of China's evolving e-commerce industry, the first systematic and comprehensive e-commerce indicator report in China, the "2000 CII China E-commerce Index Report", was officially unveiled by the China Internet Institute (CII) on 8 August 2000. It was found that the trading cost of e-commerce is 11.6% lower than that of traditional ones; trading is also 19.3% faster.[105] It was also reported that although China's e-commerce industry has good prospects, its profits are generally unsatisfactory. This is because China's acquisition of information lags behind the development of information technology, its marketing lags behind manufacturing, its application lags behind technology, and its demand lags behind supply. Exorbitant operating cost is another reason. Furthermore, the Report has listed Beijing, Guangdong, Shanghai, Tianjin and Sichuan as top regions for rapid e-commerce development in future.[106]

In China today, although some 70% of the large and medium enterprises have Internet access, most have yet to try out e-commerce.[107] They merely set up a homepage and list their e-mail addresses, mainly for the purpose of advertisement; some even do not bother to update their websites. For e-commerce to flourish, all enterprises should actively participate in the development

---

[105]The data for the report came from two sources: CII's own online surveys and information collected by Hulianwang Zhoukan (China Netweek) through its market surveys and official data provided by the State Statistics Bureau. The goal of the report is to provide objective, authoritative and accessible data on China's e-commerce development, independent of the government and any enterprises. See "China's first e-commerce index report unveiled", *Chinaonline* (11 August 2000).

[106]*Ibid.*

[107]"China Ministries Setup B2B Website: Business Websites Surveyed", *Beijing Evening Post* (8 February 2000).

of e-commerce, and not just leave it solely to the Internet Service Providers (ISPs) and Internet Content Providers (ICPs). Thus, the government's next priority is to promote B2B e-commerce.[108]

With the introduction of WAP (wireless application protocol) services, many Chinese users can soon skip the PC connectivity with direct access to the Internet via their mobile phones. The number of Chinese mobile phone users is expected to grow from the current 60 million to 100 million in 2003, of which half will be using WAP mobile phones.[109] By 2002, more people are expected to access the Internet through their mobile phones than through their PCs.[110] For those who do not have a computer but use wireless devices, WAP would enable them to conduct transactions like shopping or placing orders online. This is also known as m-commerce (mobile commerce). MeetChina.com, a Chinese e-commerce website, in co-operation with Legend and Motorola,

---

[108]In this regard, the Ministry of Foreign Trade and Economic Cooperation (MOFTEC) and the Ministry of Information Industry (MII) established a B2B e-commerce website (http://www.chinab2b.com) in mid-1999 to develop advanced e-commerce capability to facilitate and expand trade between China and other countries. Furthermore, on 26 January 2000, China's State Economic and Trade Commission (SETC), the MII and the Ministry of Science and Technology jointly established the China B2B Commerce website (http://www.chinabbc.com.cn) to lay the foundation for a B2B e-commerce environment in China. In late 1999, 11 hi-tech enterprises at Beijing's Zhongguan Cun — Legend, Founder, Stone, Great Wall, Tsinghua Tongfang, Chinet, Hope, UFsoft, Kingdee, Sangda, and Huawei — also signed up with Capital Information Development to explore the possibility of encouraging more enterprises to go online.

[109]"Motorola Partnership in Push for Mobile Banking", *South China Morning Post* (7 September 2000).

[110]*Ibid.*

has signed an agreement to broadcast its e-commerce format to wireless communication devices in China.[111] Since April 2000, the Industrial and Commercial Bank of China has started providing banking services to mobile phone users using a subscriber identity module (SIM) card.[112] Currently, almost half a million subscribers of China Mobile can access their bank accounts via mobile phones for banking services such as checking bank balances, transferring funds between accounts and paying phone bills.[113] Furthermore,

---

[111]On 29 June 2000, the first online securities order was placed over a WAP cell phone in China via GoTrade.com's GoTrade Mobile Brokerage Technology (GMBT). The GMBT Total Service Solution is a new wireless securities trading platform provided by GoTrade.com, China Unicom, China Mobile Communications Corp. and local mobile communications companies. It allows investors to make online securities transactions anytime via ordinary cellular phones, WAP cellular phones, Web-TV, pagers and other mobile communications tools. The main functions of the service include commissioned online transactions, such as order placement, and balance and transaction inquiries. The basic information services include financial and stock market information, graphs and analysis, online stock commentaries and personalized services. See "First Online Securities Trade Completed Over Cell Phone In China", *Chinaonline* (7 July 2000), http://www.chinaonline.com.

[112]"Motorola Partnership in Push for Mobile Banking", *South China Morning Post* (7 September 2000).

[113]Collaborating with 3 leading banks in China, namely, the Bank of China, the Industrial and Commercial Bank of China and China Merchants Bank, China Mobile Communications Corp., China's largest mobile network operator, recently began offering mobile banking services throughout 17 provinces and municipalities to its half million subscribers in the initial phase. See China Council for the Promotion of International Trade & China Chamber of International Commerce: China Provides Mobile Banking Services, *Trade Promotion Issue 12* (15 June 2000).

Chinese consumers can now also use their mobile phones to buy books.[114]

Most Chinese companies at present lack conspicuous advantages in their e-commerce efforts. As part of its socialist legacy, China's distributive trade sector is still very inefficient. Not many Chinese department stores have the required expertise to run retail business or to handle consumers well. If they already had problems in conventional retail business, they are unlikely to do any better in e-business. On top of this are the legal constraints in terms of effective legal protection of the various parties concerned, and the technological constraint in terms of China's still relatively backward IT infrastructure.

What has come as a surprise to the outside world is that China's e-commerce, against all these institutional and technological odds (which will be examined in detail later), should have developed so rapidly. Accordingly, many foreign and Chinese observers are optimistic about its future growth potential. Once China has strengthened the legal framework for e-commerce and sorted out the payment system (which will be discussed later), its e-commerce is set to grow much faster. Books, home electronics, laser discs, computer software and hardware, and various telecommunications equipment will remain popular·online merchandise; service products like online airline ticketing and online distance learning also hold further growth potential. China's accession to WTO is expected to boost the overall development of e-commerce in China.

---

[114]China's Dangdang Online Bookstore, which offers more than 200,000 books in Chinese, recently joined forces with linktone.com, the country's first wireless access protocol (WAP) portal, to provide Internet users with a wireless online channel for buying books. Dangdang will take advantage of linktone.com's edge over its competitors in WAP technologies and channels to offer through Dangdang's Wireless Shopping Mall services such as bestseller lists, recommendations on new and special books, and the option of browsing book catalogues.

As e-commerce in China is still at its nascent stage, centring around B2C, the B2B stage — the more profitable form of e-commerce — is not yet widespread. The structure of China's e-commerce is generally in line with the international pattern whereby B2B dominates up to 70% of total e-commerce turnover, with B2C and C2C accounting for the rest. In terms of the number of transactions, however, B2C dominates. It is believed that while B2C is revolutionary, B2B is evolutionary. Though B2C dominates in number of transactions, the volume of turnover it generates is limited. While current B2B transactions lag behind in numbers, the potential it offers vastly surpasses B2C. Unlike B2C, a single B2B transaction can spawn a huge turnover. In addition, it is estimated that the migration to B2B could generate 5–10% initial cost savings across different industries.[115]

With China zooming into the e-commerce era, the significance of cyber-branding or e-branding will gradually outgrow the importance of traditional branding or marketing. However, many Chinese, handicapped by their poor English language ability, still cannot spell correctly such famous commercial brands as Boeing, Daimler-Benz, Legend and Haier. This has severely affected the international business development strategy of these companies in the Chinese market as consumers frequently key in incorrectly spelt names and fail to access websites of these companies.[116]

---

[115]Goldman Sachs, "China: Longer Road But Bigger Payoff", *B2B E-commerce/ Internet Asia Pacific* (26 June 2000).

[116]The Boeing jet (or *Bo-yin* in Chinese) and the "Mercedes car" (called *Bian-shi*) are household names; but less than 10% of the Chinese can spell them correctly. See the paper presented by Jiang, X. P., "Economic Globalization and Cyber-branding Strategy On Different Culture And Language", at the "Conference on China's WTO Accession and Its Impact on Northeast Asia" (28–29 June 2000), Seoul, Korea. The event was organized by the Korea-China Economic Forum.

Accordingly, many big international companies are currently stepping up their efforts to promote their brands online in China.

In China, many online consumers are evidently driven by its novelty, and average B2C transaction value tends to be very small. Though B2C operators generally can save both on high rentals for their premises and from hiring sales staff, they nonetheless have to spend lavishly on advertising in order to get noticed and to create a commercial presence. (American B2Cs have to spend an average of US$300 to attract an additional customer.[117]) This, along with a number of technical and institutional constraints, will continue to limit the growth potential of B2C. On the other hand, B2B holds greater promise for future growth. On account of China's large physical size, B2B can actually facilitate inter-provincial trade.

IT Financial Infrastructure

China's rapid progress in financial reform and the modernization of its financial services in recent years have inadvertently paved the way for the subsequent development of e-commerce. The case in point are the "Golden projects", which have been particularly conducive to the growth of e-commerce. During the early 1990s, the Chinese government launched several "Golden projects" to spearhead IT growth and to promote IT applications in the mainland. For instance, the Golden Bridge project is aimed at wiring millions of Chinese citizens to the nation-wide financial network by 2010. The Golden Card project aims to facilitate national financial transactions and payments by creating a bank-card network akin to the global Cirrus networks and building regional switch centres to link ATMs and point-of-sales machines of different banks within

---

[117]"Massive costs make B2C a bad word", *The Straits Times* (7 July 2000).

regions. Furthermore, the regional centres would be linked to a national network, hence simplifying the online payment process.

Major banks in China have also been taking concrete steps to promote e-banking, even though it is still a relatively new concept to the Chinese people. The new online banking system relies on Internet and telephone technologies to conduct business instead of bank counters. It includes 24-hour customer bank account access, and allows transactions between accounts, personal financing consultation, fee payments, online shopping and online stock trading. In 1999, approximately 250,000 online securities trading accounts were opened in China though online trading volume still accounted for a minuscule 1% of the total market trade volume. In future, however, online trading volume is expected to grow over 200% annually.[118]

In August 1999, the China Construction Bank announced the provision of Internet banking services and established a national integrated business network, incorporating state-of-the-art information services and network technologies that support real-time online settlements of accounts, online shopping and other e-commerce services. Within the network, customers can manage their current accounts, fixed deposits and credit card accounts online. Advanced coding technology ensures the security of online banking services provided by the bank.[119]

In February 2000, China's largest commercial bank, the Industrial and Commercial Bank of China (ICBC owns 8.1 million enterprise accounts) expanded its online banking business to

---

[118]"Homeway Unveils New Platform for Online Securities Trade", *Business Daily* (7 August 2000).
[119]"Online Trading Needs Improvement in China", *China Daily Business Weekly* (12–18 September 2000).

enterprises throughout China, and will soon start personal online banking.[120]

In May 2000, China's central bank, the People's Bank of China (PBOC), established administrative procedures to approve online banking. Plans are also under way for the State Development Bank (SDB) to build an e-bank connected to the global network, with wholesale services as its core function. It is expected that by the year 2004, China will be the largest online banking market in Asia.[121]

E-commerce Websites and Major Players

Shortly after the emergence of the Internet, e-commerce entered the Chinese market, with the first online transaction conducted in 1996.[122] In 1998 and 1999, China only had 100 and 600 websites applying e-commerce, respectively. However, by March 2000, this mushroomed to 1,100 websites (out of about 16,000 websites). (See List 1.) Of these, 800 are online shopping sites, 100 are for online auction, 180 for online correspondence courses, and 20 for online medical care.[123] On average, 2 online stores are established per day.[124]

Of the shopping sites, one-third carry out traditional retail operations while two-thirds offer solely online services. This is in

---

[120]"Bank Boosts Online Services", *China Daily* (22 June 2000).

[121]"By the year 2004, China will be the biggest online banking market in Asia", *Brokat Infosystems AG* (26 April 2000), http://www.brokat.com/int/netnews/china-2004.html.

[122]"E-commerce In China: The CCIDnet Survey", *CCIDnet.com* (27 April 2000), http://www.ccidnet.com.

[123]*Ibid.*

[124]"Two Online Stores Born In China Everyday", *Chinaonline* (27 January 2000), http://www.chinaonline.com.

List 1 Popular E-commerce Websites in China

---

http://www.sina.com.cn

http://www.netease.com

http://www.8848.com

http://www.sohu.com.cn

http://www.163.net

http://www.263.net

http://cn.yahoo.com

http://www.soyou.com

http://www.homeway.com.cn

http://www.yabuy.com

http://www.eachnet.com

http://www.yaheal.com

http://www.focuschina.com

http://www.clubciti.com

http://www.joyed.com

http://www.xinnet.com.cn

http://www.21b-b.com

http://www.eastshop.net.cn

http://www.cpcw.com

http://www.cww.com

Source: "Internet Business In China: Current Situation and Development", *Conference on China's WTO Accession and Its Impact Impact on Northeast Asia*, Korea-China Economic Forum (28–29 June 2000).

sharp contrast to the growth of e-commerce in other countries. In Europe, for example, two-thirds of online shops operate traditional retail businesses. This indicates that China's traditional retailers are not yet as enthusiastically involved in providing online goods and services.[125]

Among the various e-commerce websites, online bookstores were the first to emerge. At present, China reportedly has more than 300 online bookstores. During the first half of 2000, the nation's total online bookstores increased by 258% compared to the same period last year. The rapid growth could be attributed to the relatively small investment required to establish an e-bookstore. The total investment in the more than 300 online stores amounts to less than 10 million yuan.[126]

Nearly 70% of China's online bookstores offer comprehensive services, including answering inquiries and taking orders for various types of books, as well as audio and video products. The remaining 30% offer information and services for books in specialized fields. In terms of size, 57% of China's online bookstores stock between 10,000 and 50,000 titles, while only 6% of them carry at least 100,000 titles. This means most of the country's bookstores are not large in scale. Currently, while 80% of the country's online bookstores practise only B2C e-commerce, 16% simultaneously practise both B2C and B2B e-commerce. Only 4% are true B2B e-bookstores.[127]

Following the emergence of e-bookstores, general merchandise has also gone online. 8848.com was the first to set up an online mall, followed by auction sites such as Netease.com, Sohu.com, Yabuy.com and Eachnet.com. Next, China's most popular portal, Sina.com, shifted its business strategy to e-commerce by opening a

---

[125]"E-commerce in China: The CCIDnet Survey", *CCIDnet.com* (27 April 2000), http://www.ccidnet.com.

[126]"Online Bookstores Grow Rapidly", *Press and Publishing News* (28 July 2000).

[127]*Ibid.*

shopping mall in its premises. The construction of most e-commerce websites are generally carried out by large enterprises, as smaller enterprises (which account for almost 90% of China's total number of enterprises) are technically not well-equipped for e-commerce.[128] Currently, most of China's e-commerce players are new companies.

E-commerce ventures in China are generally of two types. They are either established companies with an online sales component or those existing exclusively for online operations. They may be both wholesalers and retailers. Online shopping can also be specialized. For instance, yaheal.com sells drugs online as its core business, while joyed.com merely sells CDs. Others focus on PCs and computer equipment. More than 150,000 types of goods are reportedly available online.[129]

Major industry players in e-commerce include focuschina.com, the Lalashou e-commerce website; 8848.com, an online supermarket operated by Federal Software; Sina.com, an online shopping centre with 3.1 million registered users[130] offering a broad range of goods such as computer hardware, televisions, software, games, toys, books, CD-roms, gifts, cosmetics, greeting cards, washing machines, air conditioners, and shoes; Sohu.com, a network company which rents much of its space to third parties;[131] and such ISPs/ICPs as Eachnet.com, Netease.com, Xinnet.com, Yabuy.com, and Clubciti.com, all of which operate online auctions. These pioneering

---

[128]"E-commerce urged to speed up development", *China Economic News No. 49 Vol. XX* (20 December 1999).

[129]"E-commerce with Chinese Characteristics", *Chinaonline*, http://www.chinaonline.com.

[130]"Untapped Asian Market Offers Huge Potential", *South China Morning Post* (13 June 2000).

[131]For example, Motorola offers its cellular phones on the site, Compaq offers its PCs, and Intel offers Pentium 3 microchips via Sohu.com.

network companies have been quick in capitalizing on the opportunities brought about by e-commerce.

Specifically, 8848.com, launched in March 1999, is China's most popular and also most successful online shopping site. In April 1999, its sales amounted to only 400,000 yuan; but by November 1999, its monthly sales increased thirty-fold to over 12 million yuan. Today, 8848.com offers products from 300 affiliated e-stores in over 160 cities nationwide. Besides providing cash-on-delivery services, 8848.com also collaborated with China Courier Service Corporation to jointly start the Electronic Monetary System (EMS). The EMS is a payment-collection-cum-delivery system that supports electronic cash payments and provides doorstep delivery services.

China's first e-commerce service provider (ESP), Beijing Changjiang Information Company, was established in Beijing in April 2000 to offer e-commerce solutions to traditional enterprises. Their services include building, creating or designing an online business or transforming a website into an online store.[132] With more than 40 platforms and networks across China, this company deals with service activities, agriculture, commerce, and manufacturing industries. It provides solutions to numerous telecommunications, industrial and commercial enterprises.

Some e-commerce providers, in addition to selling goods online, lease some space on their websites to traditional wholesalers and retailers so that offline stores can operate their online shops in the same "cyber building". Soyou.com has about 35 retailers or companies "residing" in its "New Products" site and 22 shops taking up space in its "Discount Products" site.

---

[132]The main purpose of e-commerce solutions is to propel mortar and brick businesses (businesses which have not gone online) into e-business.

Most established IT firms such as IBM, Hewlett-Packard, Sparkice, Microsoft, Founder, Legend, China Great Wall Corp. and Sun Microsystems are, in varying degrees, already involved in e-business. Besides IT firms, large domestic enterprises like China Everbright and Midea have also started e-commerce. China's Lian Hua Supermarket established an e-commerce company in Shanghai on 20 March 2000 to develop B2B and B2C e-commerce. By integrating three networks: telephone shopping, Internet shopping and cable network shopping, Lian Hua hopes to transform its third retail revolution (i.e. forming chain stores) into a fourth retail revolution (i.e. establishing networked stores).

The China Ocean Shipping Company (COSCO) has also launched a network company, known as China Ocean Shipping Network Company, to provide global e-commerce transportation, distribution and communications network, with a start-up investment of 165 million yuan.[133] Electronic purchasing functions for the shipping business, storage and container transportation transactions, and other commercial functions will soon be introduced.

Last but not least, despite China's current ban on foreign investment on Internet firms, an American firm, Enreach Technology, launched its "FocusChina" e-commerce website on 16 September 1999. The site supplies news, multimedia and other portal services.

Methods of Payment and Delivery

It may be stressed that many of China's e-commerce websites are not purely e-commerce sites in their proper definition. Although

---

[133]The COSCO Group will gradually transfer its worldwide transportation, distribution and communications resources to the network company, which will offer a global transportation network, distribution network, global IP (Internet protocol) Internet communications network and a global distribution virtual bank.

many operators can take orders and accept payment online, most Chinese shoppers order online but pay offline. Online payment is not as popular among consumers and operators. Even website operators or vendors themselves prefer offline cash payment as several e-commerce websites have been found to accept cash-on-delivery only.[134] Various methods of payment such as online payment by credit/debit cards, online payment by bank/cash cards, payment upon delivery, payment by postal remittance, and payment via bank transfers and "electronic wallets" are practised in China (See Box 4).

Nonetheless, according to a survey conducted by the China Internet Network Information Centre (CNNIC) in mid-2000, only about one-third of online shoppers has used online payment. Nearly 40% of shoppers still prefer the traditional method of payment upon delivery, while some 20% and 18% pay through credit or debit cards and postal remittance, respectively.[135] The most common method is payment upon delivery, which overcomes the online payment barriers, particularly the cumbersome authentication process. Chinese customers are also much more comfortable with this method. However, this particular mode of payment hinders the efficient use of funds, increases operational risks and therefore increases costs to consumers. For e-commerce to take off in China, consumers must be accustomed to online payment.

China's e-commerce payment problem has not been the lack of "plastic". In fact, Chinese banks have issued more than 150 million bank cards,[136] mostly debit cards. However, the use of such cards has been hampered by business rivalries between banks and

---

[134]"Online Trading Needs Improvement in China", *China Daily Business Weekly* (12–18 September 1999).

[135]Zhongguo Hulian Wangluo Fazhan Zhuang Kuang Tongji, *Zhongguo Hulian Wangluo Xinxi Zhongxin* (Beijing, July 2000), http://www.cnnic.net.cn.

[136]"Linking Up", *Far Eastern Economic Review* (24 August 2000).

Box 4 Methods of Payment for E-commerce Transactions in China

Methods of Payment	Description
Online payment by credit or debit cards	Consumers can pay by using credit cards such as VISA, MasterCard, American Express and Diner's Club. In this case, payment can be made online globally. Credit cards or debit cards issued by Chinese banks such as the Bank of China, the Industrial and Commercial Bank of China, and the China Merchant Bank are accepted but limited to selected cities across China. Some examples are the China Merchant Bank's Yikatong and Yiwangtong card systems, the Bank of China's Great Wall electronic debit card and Great Wall renminbi credit card, the China Construction Bank's Long card and the Agricultural Bank of China's Golden Ear of Grain card. Of these options, the China Merchant Bank's Yiwangtong system is the most popular for online payments.
Online payment by bank cards	Another method of payment is via bank cards, or rather, savings account cards issued by the Chinese banks such as the Construction Bank of China, the Industrial and Commercial Bank of China and the Shanghai Pudong Development Bank. The verification process takes as long as 15 days before delivery can be made.
Payment upon delivery	This is the method which most Chinese prefer. Nonetheless, this method is limited to selected cities. For instance, <u>8848.net</u> makes this option available only to 19 cities. Payment upon delivery can also be collected by couriers such as EMS or DHL.
Payment by bank transfers	Consumers can pay by transferring funds from their accounts to the online operators' accounts. This could mean global online account transfers or nationwide online account transfers.
Postal remittance	Payment can also be in the form of postal remittance where consumers pay via the post office.
Payment by electronic wallets	Consumers can pay using electronic wallets issued by some commercial banks, which is available in certain provinces.

incompatible equipment. Before recent innovations, consumers could only use their cards only for selective online purchasers from websites that had individual agreements with specific local banks. Recently, online payment has been made easy under an integrated nation-wide payment system.

On 9 June 2000, ChinaPay.com launched a new website payment system, which offers the "OneLinkPay" system, providing instant verification services for consumers wishing to make online purchases. Rather similar to the credit card authentication systems in developed countries, "OneLinkPay" confirms transactions in less than 30 seconds and enables businesses to receive payment within 24 hours, resulting in faster fulfilment of order than with other systems currently in use in China. Under this system, Chinese banks, businesses and consumers are inter-linked to access a single, secure and real-time online payment system that can handle more than 150 million bank cards in China.

ChinaPay.com's application service provider (ASP) model simplifies the payment process by allowing businesses to link up with the national bank card network by renting ChinaPay.com's payment software. With this service, consumers are not limited to use just one or two specific bank cards but a multiple range of bank cards, when paying online. Besides key industry players such as Eachnet.com and Homeway.com.cn, China Ocean Shipping Co. (COSCO) has also reached an agreement to use the service for their B2B transactions.

As for the delivery of merchandise, methods can vary from one operator to another. Some team up with the post office by using the regular postal service to reach out to the entire nation. Others link up with chain stores to go beyond their primary line of business. Still more, some link up with domestic express delivery carriers, the delivery arm of EMS, and foreign giants such as DHL, to offer local delivery within 24 to 48 hours. Currently, the postal service and EMS are the most common methods of delivery in China.[137] However, non-physical "service products" such as CDs and software and online correspondence courses can be delivered directly online.

Issues and Obstacles

Economic Issues

E-commerce is supposed to provide a more convenient service and offer lower prices than traditional commerce. However, e-commerce overheads, including the start-up costs and funds needed to maintain and promote the websites, can be astronomical. It can cost from US$400,000 to US$1 million just to keep a site.[138] Hence, a large volume of business is required to support the logistics and overhead costs. Keeping costs down and maintaining reasonable profit margins are currently the main challenges faced by e-commerce operators in China. To be able to survive, an e-commerce operator has to spend a lot of costly promotion and marketing money to expand its scale and build up its presence even before it starts earning any revenue. Worse still, e-commerce clients are usually not loyal customers.[139] Not surprisingly, many Internet

---

[137]EMS is common because it can remit payments in just 7 days, as compared to the monthly settlement of credit card bills. Furthermore, EMS promises to refund the online vendor or return undelivered goods so that the threat of consumer fraud is greatly reduced.

[138]"Grim forecast for bulk of cash-strapped online firms", *South China Morning Post* (23 June 2000).

[139]It was reported that in 1998, 5 sites spent 2.5 million yuan (US$300,000) on promotion, whilst in 1999, 13 sites spent 65 million yuan (US$7.8 million) on marketing. It is estimated that 15 sites are planning to spend 750 million yuan (US$90 million) on advertising campaigns in 2000. See "E-commerce With Chinese Characteristics", *Chinaonline*, http://www.chinaonline.com.

companies are fuelling an advertising boom in the offline world by placing ads on buses and bus shelters.[140]

Currently, most of China's Internet companies are cash-strapped, especially after the dotcom fever has subsided. Information Industry Minister Wu Jichuan recently predicted that 70–80% of China's Internet companies would fold up unless they could obtain new credit from banks.[141] This points to another problem hindering the growth of the sector — China's financial sector. E-commerce requires strong financial support from the banking sector. It also needs new financial services, such as an interbank credit card system and an electronic wallet system. At present, there is no effective nation-wide financial network in China; nor has the financial industry become fully electronic. E-banking, as mentioned earlier, is still at its infancy in China. Thus, e-commerce cannot continue to grow while the financial sector lags behind. Furthermore, purchasing options outside China are limited by foreign exchange restrictions.

Of the numerous e-commerce operators, only 8848.com boasts a relatively complete system for supporting various methods of payment. In 1999, China Merchants Bank launched a pilot programme to issue cards in selected cities allowing renminbi payments online.[142] Although the China Merchants Bank has invested substantially in online payment and other online banking services, its revenue from online services is still negligible.

---

[140]"China Online Start-Ups Hop on Ad Bus", *The Asian Wall Street Journal* (4 July 2000).

[141]"Grim Forecast for Bulk of Cash-strapped Online Firms", *South China Morning Post* (23 June 2000).

[142]China Merchants Bank announced the launch of its online banking services in September 1999, with the debut of corporate and retail banking, online securities trading and online payment.

Technical Issues

China's network infrastructure is still underdeveloped, and is unable to handle a high volume of e-commerce transactions efficiently. The network transmission speeds are not only slow but also unreliable, which has been frustrating to both e-businesses and individuals. The Internet exit bandwidth in China is less than 200 Mbps, even less than the exit bandwidth of the U.S. company, Intel. The United States had developed a good IT infrastructure before e-commerce became popular. But the situation is just the opposite in China, where increasing demand for e-commerce is driving the upgrading and expansion of IT infrastructure.

Furthermore, China's transportation networks of roads and railways are also backward. The railway system is overloaded while roads, including the expressways, are often congested. This hampers EMS and intra-city express delivery services, which are presently the prime methods of delivery. China's other popular method of delivery is through the post office. But the postal system in China is also slow and uncertain in its deliveries.

By common international standards, services provided by e-commerce websites/companies in China are inefficient and slow. Many websites do not provide "24/7 service" (24 hours a day for 7 days a week). Some websites can only confirm orders on business days — a working week in China has only 5 days. Friction between website administrators and their suppliers or distributors is common. Many e-commerce companies/websites have to resort to traditional form of communications like telephone to sort out problems with their suppliers and distributors. In short, many operators have yet to reap the full e-commerce efficiency based on completely computerized distribution channels.

Such slow and uncertain services inevitably undermine the credibility of e-commerce companies/websites. Except for some major industry players such as 8848.com, Star Store and Shanghai Meilin, all having developed a relatively mature distribution system, China's other e-commerce operators do not have the experience and management resources to handle this completely new line of business. Many disgruntled consumers have been accordingly put off, and they have returned to traditional shopping rather than waiting for the long delivery of goods.[143] According to a survey conducted in mid-2000, 22% users complained that they never received the goods they ordered and paid for online.[144]

Apart from the start-up difficulty mentioned above, many of the problems are clearly attributable to the systemic inefficiency in China's distributive trade and transportation sectors. The next phase of China's e-commerce development, therefore, critically depends on not just the upgrading of its IT infrastructure, but also the much-needed modernization of its inefficient distributive trade. Specifically, one immediate priority is to speed up the development of a reasonably high-quality "express delivery" service (similar to the United Parcel Service in USA), which is equipped to handle common e-commerce items like software, computers, books and cosmetics.

Social Issues

Admittedly, China's consumer e-commerce is still in its early stages. Although the number of Internet users in China has been increasing rapidly, the base is still very small, especially so in e-commerce

---

[143]"E-commerce in China: The CCIDnet Survey", *CCIDnet.com* (27 April 2000), http://www.ccidnet.com.

[144]Zhongguo Hulian Wangluo Fazhan Zhuang Kuang Tongji, *Zhongguo Hulian Wangluo Xinxi Zhongxin* (Beijing, July 2000), http://www.cnnic.net.cn.

where only a small proportion of Internet users readily embrace the new form of commerce. With such a small number of core online shoppers, e-commerce in China naturally cannot prosper based on the economies of scale.

The mindset of Chinese consumers is also a crucial factor for e-commerce to flourish. The lack of personal relationships and contacts or the much-cherished *guanxi* in online commerce has been a hindrance to the development of B2B e-commerce. *Guanxi* has played a major role in most successful business deals in China. Such relationships are especially crucial in the information-poor environment with a weak legal framework. Most companies actually do not like the idea of conducting business with new partners without any personal contact, given the lack of corporate and credit information. The problem is aggravated by an extremely fragmented market with too many industry players and the difficulty in implementing binding contracts. Furthermore, to develop such *guanxi*, corruption is usually involved. In China, it is common for suppliers to reward their customers with gifts or monetary payoffs. However, with online commerce, *guanxi* cannot be readily established electronically nor the rewards of gifts or money be given easily.

Driven primarily by novelty and convenience, China's online shoppers had originally high expectations of website services. In their choice of an e-commerce website, they would naturally prefer those that meet their basic requirements, such as fast browsing and convenient searches. Value-added services (product recommendations, news releases and free software downloads, etc.) are still not among Chinese consumers' major considerations, however. Consumers prefer to shop online for small commodities that are relatively inexpensive and low-risk like books, CDs and software, which do not require post-sales service or speedy delivery.

In fact, most transactions are so small that they hardly need to go online. But it is these small and low-risk commodity items that currently constitute the bulk of the e-commerce transactions in China. The same phenomenon is also true of other Asian societies at their initial phase of e-commerce.

Online shopping, on account of having to pay in advance, the lack of face-to-face contact and the "invisibility" of the transaction site, has to depend heavily on consumer trust and the credibility of the websites. This poses a problem for China where the post-sales service is poor or non-existent; the legal protection of consumers is inadequate; and there is virtually no credible consumer movement. Though the popularity of the Internet and mobile phones has fast changed the social outlook of urban China, a distinct e-commerce culture has yet to take root.

Not surprisingly, most consumers are sceptical about online shopping, and they still prefer the traditional mode of shopping: to see, touch, hear, taste, and smell the merchandise so as to ensure product quality prior to purchase. The limits of online purchasing by individuals lie in the fact that it can only complement traditional retailing, not to displace shopping in stores. Above all, China's existing traditional retail network in urban areas, with its ubiquitous corner shops, wet and dry markets, and hawkers, has served its resident consumers very well, being all located within walking distance. There is, strictly speaking, no compelling reason for residents to resort to online shopping at China's present stage of development. Hence, up till today, only some 14% of China's Internet users have tried out online shopping.

E-commerce operators also need to entice more women to go online to join the digital commercial revolution since presently, most Internet users in China are male. The older people have also not been left out. Recently, with the support of the Beijing Municipal government, a website was set up to encourage the elderly residents to apply e-commerce to their daily lives by shopping online.[145]

Recent Developments

In October 1999, China's first e-commerce Agricultural Wholesale Online Market started operation in Guangdong. The site is a joint project developed by the provincial government and IBM. In addition to order-based transactions, the new website will be equipped to handle online electronic transactions, including long-distance transactions.

On 15 October 1999, the Zhejiang Daily offered its first online subscription service. In China, although it is not unusual for newspapers to have web pages with subscription information, Zhejiang Daily's move made it the first newspaper company to allow online payment.

On 5 April 2000, China's first B2B2C e-commerce website was established, when the Wang Zhi company formally went online in Beijing with the debut of a vertical website group service concept. Four of its websites namely, the Stepone Network, the Doctor World Network, the Beat 100 Network and the My House website combined to form this group. The group will adopt purchasing, merger, cooperation and alliance methods to expand their business.

In May 2000, China's advertising regulator, the State Administration of Industry and Commerce, issued 27 pilot online

---

[145]Residents are encouraged to buy goods and services via a website at http://www.hhl.com.cn. So far, purchases include daily households needs such as potatoes, cooking oil and packets of salt. Residents can also obtain services such as baby-sitting and home appliance repair via the website. See "Beijing Website Serves Elderly Shoppers", *China Daily Business Weekly* (2–8 July 2000).

advertising licenses to domestic e-commerce operators, such as Netease.com and Sohu.com, to conduct online advertising. In view of the low levels of sales revenue, most e-commerce operators depend on advertising income for funding.[146] The move was warmly welcomed by industry players.

E-commerce has also reached China's West. In May 2000, Ningxia was picked to be the launchpad for Western China's first e-commerce port. It will be built under the supervision of world-famous high-tech companies such as Compaq and Oracle. With the establishment of the port, goods, funds and information in Western China can be traded in that region. This will allow large commodity trading houses in Chongqing, Chengdu, Kunming, Nanning, Xi'an, Lanzhou, Xining, Yinchuan, Lhasa, Urumqi and Hohhot to obtain the best procurement prices.

In June 2000, the China Internet Network Information Center (CNNIC) and China Enterprises (http://www.ce.net.cn) agreed to jointly develop a programme to train Chinese businesses in e-commerce.[147] In addition, CNNIC will annually conduct a standardized test nationwide and issue certificates to individuals qualified for e-commerce, setting up objective and reliable standards according to which companies may choose their e-commerce talents.

In July 2000, the research subsidiary of China's Ministry of Communications, in collaboration with Winsan (China) Investment Group, linked up the country's isolated regional logistics systems

---

[146]In 1999, Netease.com drew 65% of its US$2 million revenue from advertising; whilst Sohu.com drew 93% of its US$1.6 million from advertising. See "China Issues 27 Licenses for Internet Advertising", *The Asian Wall Street Journal* (1 June 2000).

[147]"New Program to Train China Companies in E-commerce", *Xinhua News Agency* (8 June 2000).

online to raise transport service standards and bolster domestic trade.[148]

On 13 July 2000, the first website providing comprehensive services to managers — My Managers Club — was established. This website is targetted at senior and middle management and professionals from state-owned, privately operated and foreign enterprises, providing online consultation, training and news. Through close co-operation with professional consultation companies, educational institutions and business associations, the website has built a broad platform for exchange and co-operation among businesses, creating a B2C2B operation mode.

On 19 July 2000, China's first parenting website, GoodBaby.com, went into operation. GoodBaby, which is one of the largest business groups specializing in the design, manufacture and sale of baby products, received direct investment from the U.S. International Group and US$10 million in venture capital from the subsidiary of Softbank Group (Japan) for the website.[149] The investors will jointly enter the e-commerce business, providing children's products through GoodBaby.com.

On 25 July 2000, some of the world's largest and famous corporations, including Microsoft Corp., General Motors Corp., United Parcel Service (UPS), IBM and Intel, banded together to influence the formation of e-commerce regulations in China. On this day, the group announced the establishment of the E-commerce China Forum (ECCF), a coalition comprising 36 international and

---

[148]The official website, Transonline, will be launched in August 2000, to enable freight information exchanges and online business among manufacturers, buyers and transport and warehousing companies. See "Freight Efficiency Improved Online", *South China Morning Post* (10 July 2000).

[149]"Baby Steps: China's First Parenting Website Goes Into Operation", *Beijing Evening News* (20 July 2000).

Chinese companies from diverse e-commerce-related industries, to promote a policy and industry environment that supports the development of e-commerce in China. The group seeks to work with the government in the development of industry standards and regulations by taking a cooperative approach. A broad range of e-commerce issues in China, including investment, content, encryption, online taxation, advertising, payment, and security privacy are expected to be addressed.

ECCF currently has committees focused on security and encryption, infrastructure and Internet service providers, payment and financing, fulfillment and distribution, business to business, content and Internet content providers (ICPs), and legal issues. At present, ECCF has 36 member companies from around the world, including China, North America, Europe and Asia. Founding members include America Online, Asia Connect, Baker & McKenzie, Cable & Wireless, ChinaNow, eCantata.com, General Motors, Hewlett-Packard, IBM, Intel, Ji Tong Communications, Legend Technology Co., Lucent Technologies, Microsoft Corp., Motorola, Samsung, Standard Chartered Bank and UPS.

In early August 2000, Homeway.com.cn formally introduced to the market the Homeway Online Trade Comprehensive Service Platform, the first in China capable of meeting the needs of both securities trading firms and investors. Via this platform, Homeway provides services including Internet access, financial information, expert commentaries, technical analysis, online trading and personalized financial services to securities companies and their customers. The service platform adopted the telecommunication industry's certificate-authority authentication system used in Beijing. Available access options include mobile phones, two-way pagers, TV set-top boxes and other terminal equipment besides computers.

On 10 August 2000, China's insurance company, Ping An Insurance, launched the first online personal injury insurance for air passengers, following a co-operation agreement with the Civil Aviation Administration of China (CAAC) and Beijing Jinhangwang Information Co. According to the agreement, CAAC's business data network would be utilized to provide air passengers with online insurance underwriting services via 28,000 computer terminals at 5,000 travel agencies across the country.[150] Furthermore, ticketing computers will be able to print out insurance policies along with air tickets, hence simplifying and speeding the ticketing and insurance process.

On 24 August 2000, the Shenzhen E-commerce Certificate Authentication Center was formally established to provide authentication of network identities for the government, enterprises, banks and individuals via its credit information system platform. Furthermore, it will become a capital and credit consultation center for organizations to protect against online theft and swindle. The Shenzhen E-commerce Certificate Authentication Center is the seventh of its kind in the country, with similar institutions already established in Beijing, Shanghai, Guangzhou and other cities.

In late August 2000, China-enterprise.com's purchaser-product-seller (PPS) platform formally began operation with the support of the Industrial and Commercial Bank of China (ICBC) and the China Merchants Bank (CMB). This is the first B2B e-business platform in China to realize secure online payment. The PPS electronic business platform, which has more than 1,000 kinds of products in 26 industries, brings together the purchaser, the product and the seller — the three basic elements of commodity trading. Its services

---

[150]"Insurance Company Offers Online Personal Injury, Air Tickets", *Chinaonline* (17 August 2000), http://www.chinaonline.com.

include searches and announcements of supply and demand information, facilitation of price negotiation and correspondence exchange, contract signing and implementation follow-up, delivery and transportation of commodities and online payment.

Large international mail-order companies are also scrambling for a slice of China's growing e-commerce market. Otto, the world's largest mail-order company, has opened a website for its Shanghai division, with more than 500 online users every day. German firms Quelle and Bertelsmann have also set up joint ventures in Shanghai. Mecox Lane, the first foreign mail-order company to set up operation in China in 1996, recently invested US$13 million to build a comprehensive website, called m18.com, for extensive e-commerce services in China.[151]

China's accession to the WTO will spur further growth of e-commerce. In allowing global Internet companies to own 49–100% of the shares of Chinese Internet companies, post-WTO China will improve its overall e-commerce environment.[152] Both local and foreign banks, shipping companies and insurance companies will have a wider scope for their e-business operations. More foreign online e-stores will be attracted to the China market on the promise of millions of potential Chinese online shoppers.[153] The Chinese side will also count on the rapid growth in the potential global demand for China's labour-intensive products via the e-commerce channel.

---

[151]"Mail-order Firms Scramble for Slice of Shanghai Market", *South China Morning Post* (4 September 2000).

[152]However, China's WTO accession will allow foreign companies to own 49–50% of shares of Chinese telecommunications companies. See "WTO Entry To Open China's E-commerce Market", *Chinaonline* (23 November 1999), http://www.chinaonline.com.

[153]*Ibid.*

It is still uncertain as to what proportion of China's international trade, currently at around US$360 billion,[154] will be handled through online trading. But foreign participation will certainly speed up the technical upgrading of China's IT infrastructure and the eventual standardization and modernization of China's e-commerce system, including the much-needed reform of China's online payment system, offline delivery, and Internet platforms. All these are currently weak links in China's e-commerce, which will take many years to remedy. The WTO membership may provide just the needed impetus.

---

[154]General Administration of Customs of the PRC, *China Customs Statistics* (January 2000).

Box 5 Legal and Regulatory Framework

Regulatory Agency/ Regulatory Environment	
Regulatory agency	The Ministry of Information Industry (MII) is the overall regulatory agency responsible for the e-commerce industry.
Associations promoting e-commerce	In September 1996, the China International Electronic Commerce Center (CIECC) was established, followed by the creation of the China International Electronic Commerce Network (CIECNet), an e-commerce network which covers the whole country and links up with the world. The initiative was a positive demonstration of China's understanding of the impact of technology on trade and commerce and its commitment to encourage and facilitate international business and investments in the IT age. On 21 June 2000, the MII launched the China Electronic Commerce Association (CECA), with Vice-Minister Lu Xingui as honorary chairman. CECA will promote the development of e-commerce via research, investigation, consulting, training and exhibition. CECA will also act as a bridge between the government and e-commerce operators.
Regulatory environment	The development of e-commerce raises issues in many other aspects such as taxation, tariff collection and an effective legal framework. China has already made important progress in both tax and legal reforms, but is still struggling to complete the process. Although there are no formal laws and regulations governing e-commerce in China, the government has recognised the importance of regulating this nascent but growing industry, which is a critical component of the new economy. Several guidelines and preliminary laws governing e-commerce in China have been issued.

Box 5 (Continued)

Guidelines/ Laws and Regulations	
The Contract Law (Excerpts)	In March 1999, China's newly adopted Contract Law embraces new concepts in the IT area, including e-commerce. The new Law introduces the concepts of "offering" and "acceptance", whereby one party sells a commodity on a website at a suggested price (offering) while another party decides to buy it (acceptance). Such an exchange legally binds the two parties into a formal contract relationship. In particular, Article 11 stipulates that the law recognizes "a memorandum of contract, letter or electronic message (including telegrams, telexes, facsimiles, electronic data exchanges and electronic mails), etc. that is capable of expressing its contents in a tangible form". Besides recognizing the concept of "electronic messages" for the first time, the law also lays down the foundation for IT network contracts. This means that electronic data exchange and e-mail can carry the legal powers of a written contract.
Guidelines On The Development Of China's E-commerce Industry	The MII issued the *Guidelines On The Development Of China's E-commerce Industry* in December 1999, aimed at developing an "e-commerce industry with Chinese characteristics" (See Annex 6).
Circular Of The Beijing Municipal Administration For Industry And Commerce Concerning E-commerce Activities Registration	On 28 March 2000, the *Circular Of The Beijing Municipal Administration For Industry And Commerce Concerning E-commerce Activities Registration* was issued by the Beijing Municipal Administration for Industry and Commerce to meet the requirements of China's Internet economic development. It also aims to differentiate and standardize business activities on the Internet, to enhance the government's sense of service, to protect the lawful rights and interests of enterprises and consumers, to crack down on illegal business activities, to maintain the socio-economic order and to establish an e-commerce operations registration system (See Annex 7).

Box 5 (Continued)

New rules on e-commerce digital certificates	In April 2000, Shanghai took a major step ahead by publishing the *New Rules On E-commerce Digital Certificates* for the Shanghai Municipality to strengthen the management of the pricing and the charges to standardize service in relation to the authentication of e-commerce digital certificates (See Annex 8).
Interim Regulations for the Online Securities Brokerage Sector	In April 2000, China released the *Interim Regulations for the Online Securities Brokerage Sector*, banning non-brokerage firms from engaging in online securities trading. This caused the firms to change their securities websites and alter their business operations accordingly. Those which originally intended to launch e-commerce operations for online trading had to re-position themselves as providers that would build e-commerce platforms for securities brokers. However, in response to the new regulations, not all of China's securities companies are changing the services they offer. Nonetheless, the new regulations are expected to have a negative impact on such firms because according to the interim provisions, securities firms will receive 100% of the commissions from securities trading, while the website operators will get nothing.
Notice on Protecting the Legitimate Rights and Interests of Consumers in Network Economic Activities	On 7 July 2000, the Beijing Municipal Administration for Industry and Commerce (BMAIC) issued a "Notice on Protecting the Legitimate Rights and Interests of Consumers in Network Economic Activities" which reiterated relevant provisions from the "Law on the Protection of Consumer Rights and Interests" and the "Law Against Unfair Competition" to protect the interests of online buyers.[155] The new notice contains specific provisions concerning events commonly associated with e-commerce, especially fraud, false advertising and offers of fake goods.

[155]"Get the Fraud Out of the Baud: Beijing Issues Laws to Regulate E-commerce", *Chinaonline* (13 July 2000).

Box 5 (Continued)

	The new law states that business operators who sell goods or offer services via websites must do the following:

The new law states that business operators who sell goods or offer services via websites must do the following:

- Provide consumers with their actual place of registration, methods of contact or the location where transactions are carried out. Business owners may not provide false addresses.
- State explicitly the price of goods to be sold or services to be offered, and not offer false prices for goods or services.
- State clearly the manufacturer, place of production and the quality of the goods offered.
- Not make misleading or false claims on websites either through advertising or by other methods.

The BMAIC's new measures additionally warns online buyers that they should look for information on websites that denotes these sites have registered legally and provides the true identity of its operators, for consumers' own protection. The BMAIC regulation also contains additional provisions:

- If Internet users notice unregistered websites, these web surfers should visit the agency's own website at hd315.gov.cn to obtain further information.
- Online businesses should give consumers purchase receipts or service vouchers in accordance to relevant regulations or business practices, and consumers should save the relevant evidence in case of disputes.
- If consumers are involved in a dispute concerning an online purchase, they may register a complaint either by e-mail at hd315.gov.cn or lodge a complaint by phone.

Box 5 (Continued)

	• Online business operators who infringe on the legitimate rights and interests of consumers by violating provisions of this notice will receive necessary punishment from the BMAIC according to relevant provisions. • The BMAIC will protect the rights and interests of consumers under the law.
Net tax	As China's current tax laws do not cover Internet transactions, the Chinese government is currently drafting rules for the taxation of e-commerce and online securities trading. The Chinese government, holding the view that e-commerce should not be treated differently from other businesses, is determined to tax e-commerce even though it may hinder Internet development. Any form of taxation would slow down or delay e-commerce's ability to earn a profit and would increase the cost of developing the entire economy. In addition, relevant government agencies are also in the process of drafting a taxation policy measure, the "Implementation of Specific Internet Taxation Rules and Regulations", to combat online tax fraud and tax evasion. Taxing e-commerce is expected to increase the cost of usage of the Internet. The government's move indicated that e-commerce has reached a certain volume that the government wants to intervene so that this business would not be kept off-limits from tax collectors. Furthermore, the government believes that in the near future, a significant part of commerce would be conducted online, and if online transactions were not taxed, a substantial amount of revenues would be lost.[156]

---

[156]"Taxman Ready To Pounce On Web Revenue", *South China Morning Post* (31 July 2000).

Box 5 (Continued)

	Businesses in China are currently taxed at a rate of 6%, based on the issuance of receipts. However, as online trading does not provide physical receipts, businesses can easily avoid paying taxes.
	Nonetheless, one major obstacle in collecting taxes from the Internet is locating taxpayers, especially in transactions of invisible commodities such as intellectual property rights and cross-border deals. Also, because e-commerce is characteristically expedient, direct, confidential and secure, there would be no direct targets to be taxed. Furthermore, as trading on the Internet is paperless, taxation is relatively difficult to carry out.
	Although the Chinese government does not wish to forgo the right to tax transactions over the Internet, it favours a preferential tax treatment in order not to hamper the development of the Internet and e-commerce.[157]
Regulation for online advertising	Legal loopholes and irregular operations in Internet advertising will be closed by new rules put into effect by the end of 2000. The new regulations would set up a market entry criterion for Internet companies which want to put up advertisements on their websites.
	The lack of regulations has made it difficult to conduct effective supervision of online advertisements, which has damaged consumers' rights by deceptive and fake advertisements.
	The new regulations are not just designed to tighten supervision or facilitate regular checks on the ads content and mode of operation, but also to encourage regular commercial practices. Under the new regulations, websites must apply for a license to list commercials. Websites, which fail to meet the set of criteria, would be prohibited from online advertising.

---

[157]"Internet to Get Tax Preferences — China Finance Minister", *Chinaonline* (17 April 2000).

Box 5 (Continued)

Regulation for online medical services	At present, the Chinese government is wrestling with the issue of how to regulate online medical services, as the Beijing Municipal Health Department (BMHP) drafts regulations governing medical services provided over the Internt.[158]
	China is estimated to have hundreds of medical websites. Except for a few capable of providing long-distance diagnoses, most of these websites offer information concerning medical treatment and health care.
	Although many of these Internet medical services are fast and convenient, hidden perils can await people who act on their recommendations. A misdiagnosis is highly possible with an "online doctor" because of deficient diagnostic procedures. Some diseases cannot be diagnosed this way, and a face-to-face examination instead is often required.
	Internet medical services are primarily consultative services. Hence, the proposed regulations indicated that Internet medical services should not use the word "hospital" and medical treatments such as outpatient and emergency-room services must be performed at medical institutions rather than over the Internet.
	To standardize medical and health care services offered over the Internet, the regulations also stipulate that people, including volunteers, providing this information online must be professionally certified. In addition, remote medical treatments will be provided by medical institutions themselves.

---

[158]"Beijing Checks Up on Net Medical Sites, Urges Certification", *Beijing Evening News* (2 August 2000).

Box 5 (Continued)

Regulation for online bookstores	In June 2000, the State Press and Publishing Bureau announced that book retailers must obtain an official operating license and register with the State Administration of Industry and Commerce before conducting business online. In order to qualify for an operating license, online booksellers must first subject to examination and approval according to state regulations governing the management of publishing operations in China. With such a regulation in place, web-based booksellers can no longer start their e-business simply by registering a domain name and setting up an e-store. Those already selling online, particularly commercial operations, will be subjected to review.
China's e-commerce strategy	At present, the Chinese government is still in the process of formulating an all-encompassing e-commerce strategy for the development of e-commerce in China. The strategy would examine issues such as problems concerning permission to enter the Chinese market and operational logistics for foreign businesses wanting to invest in China's Internet sector (including e-commerce). It would also address problems relating to e-commerce's legal and financial frameworks. The legal framework supports commercial laws, intellectual property rights or copyrights and trademarks, domain names, privacy and security, while the financial framework includes issues concerning tariffs, taxes and online payments.

Box 6 Security Issues Concerning E-commerce in China

Security Issues	
Online payment	The security of e-commerce payment transactions is a global problem, which is also a major concern of Chinese consumers. This is reflected in their worry over online companies' credibility and payment security and hence, their preference for traditional shopping and payment on delivery. In a survey, about 80% of China's Internet users believe that e-commerce provides no guaranteed replacement or payment security.[159]
Online banking/ transactions	In late 1999, the PBOC-led National Banking Certificate Authorization (CA) Centre signed several contracts with online security system suppliers to construct an Internet CA system to facilitate secure application of online transactions. Currently, the authoritative certificate recognition system has been adopted by many banks, including the CITIC Industrial Bank and ICBC. The CITIC Industrial Bank is the first to adopt certificates of newly founded China Financial Certificate Authorization Centre (CFCA) to guarantee safe online banking. The CFCA, founded by the PBOC and 12 major commercial banks in June 2000, grants certificates to e-commerce users on the basis of credit record inspection.[160]
China's first secure Internet server	In early 2000, China's first secure Internet server, the Founder Yuanming Internet Secure, was launched by the Founder Science & Technology Computer Co. This device protects business information systems and resources from outside intrusion and attack, while allowing the government to go online by ensuring the security of the government information network.

---

[159]"E-commerce In China: The CCIDnet Survey", *Chinaonline* (5 May 2000), http://www.chinaonline.com.
[160]"CITIC Industrial Offers Online Services", *South China Morning Post* (14 July 2000).

Box 6 (Continued)

	Founder Yuanming Internet Secure adopts a new mode of security, known as "active isolation". It links a business internal network with the Internet through two layers of security protection. The system both customizes the content to be transmitted to ensure the security of content and employs physical isolation to guarantee the security of the network. System managers can customize website content according to their needs, and can adopt different updating tactics, including automatic updating, regular updating and manual updating. The secure server is capable of processing requests from over 200 visitors per second.
Security authentication system	China has yet to establish an efficient security authentication system through which corporate or individual credit can be verified under security regardless of geographical location. Without such an effective security authentication system, it would be highly risky for anyone, be it business or individual, to conduct transactions online. Fears were intensified when hackers used available technology to obtain 80,000 personal credit account numbers and passwords from hacking different commercial websites in early 1998.[161] It was reported that more than 90% of China's web portals and e-commerce websites have serious security flaws.[162]

---

[161]*Ibid.*

[162]"Hack Attack: 90% of Chinese Websites Not Secure", *Guangzhou Daily* (18 May 2000).

Box 6 (Continued)

	In fact, the China Consumers Association (CCA) recently issued its eighth consumer alert of the year to warn China's Internet users to guard personal information from the websites to prevent it from being misused. The consumer association's investigations found the security of such important personal information as users' names, identification numbers, e-mail addresses and credit card numbers, which may be divulged while communicating, shopping and registering online, may be at risk. According to the CCA, Internet users' personal information can be divulged because some online operators sell customer information to third parties; some websites are not well-equipped with network security technologies and this creates an opportunity for lawbreakers and hackers. Some Internet users also unwittingly divulge their e-mail addresses while chatting online.

ANNEX 1

PRC INTERIM PROVISIONS OF THE REGULATION OF COMPUTER NETWORKS AND THE INTERNET[163]

Article 1: These ordinances strengthen regulations on computer information networks (CINs) that connect to the Internet and ensure the proper expansion of international computer information exchanges.

Article 2: CINs that connect to the Internet within the borders of the PRC should follow these regulations.

Article 3: The meanings of phrases used in these regulations

1. CTWI (CINs Connecting to the Worldwide Internet) refers to CINs within PRC borders that are connecting to foreign CINs for the purpose of facilitating international information exchange.
2. The Internet refers to the CIN directly connected to CTWI; network connecting units refer to units responsible for the operation of interconnecting networks.

---

[163]"PRC Interim Provisions on the Regulation of Computer Networks and the Internet" were issued by the Secretary Bureau of the State Council General Office on 1 February 1996. Source: "PRC Interim Provisions on the Regulation of Computer Networks and the Internet", *Chinaonline*, http://www.chinaonline.com.

3. Entering the network means connecting to the Internet's CIN through entry points; these points are controlled by entry point units.

Article 4:   With regard to connecting to the Internet, the state will act according to the objectives of establishing general plans, unifying standards, facilitating divisional management and promoting expansion.

Article 5:   The State Council's Economic Information Leadership Group (LG) is responsible for mediating and resolving major problems in CTWI work. The office of the LG will set up specific measures according to these regulations, clearly listing and explaining the rights, duties and responsibilities of units providing international information entry and exit channels, network connecting units, entry point units and users. The LG will also be responsible for the monitoring and inspection of CTWI work.

Article 6:   CINs directly completing CTWI must use the international information entry and exit channels provided by the then Ministry of Posts and Telecommunications (MPT)'s public telecom network. No unit or individual may independently establish or utilize other channels to complete CTWI.

Article 7:   Networks that are already established will be managed by the then MPT and the Ministry of Electronics Industry, or the current MII, the National Education Council, or the Chinese Academy of Sciences. New networks must be approved by the State Council.

Article 8:   Computer networks intended for connection to international computer networks should be connected via the Internet. Organizations intended to be network connecting units should report to relevant supervisory departments or units and apply for inspection and permission. When applying for inspection and permission, organizations should furnish information such as the nature of their CIN, scope of usage and necessary domain names.

Article 9:   Entry point units must have the following qualifications:

1. They must be legally established corporations or institutions.
2. They must have related CIN, equipment and technological and administrative personnel.
3. They must have a sound set of systems and procedures that ensure safety, safeguard secrecy and protect technologies.
4. They must also obey the laws and regulations of the country as well as requirements set up by the State Council.

Article 10:   Computers and other CINs belonging to individuals, legal persons and other organizations (hereafter referred to as "users" in this document) must connect to the Internet through an entry point network. They must apply for permission from the entry point unit and undergo registration procedures.

Article 11:   Units providing international information entry and exit channels, network connecting units as well as entry point units should establish related network management centres. They should strengthen regulation of their own units and users, safeguard network information security, and ensure satisfactory and safe services.

Article 12: Network connecting units and entry point units should be responsible for the technological training and managerial education of their own units and users.

Article 13: Units and individuals involved in CTWI services should obey the laws and regulations of the country and strictly comply with measures to maintain security and secrecy. No unit or individual may use the Internet to engage in criminal activities such as harming national security or disclosing state secrets. No unit or individual may use the Internet to retrieve, replicate, create, or transmit information that threatens social stability or promotes sexually suggestive material.

Article 14: Violators of Articles 6, 8, and 10 will be warned, publicly criticized, then forced to terminate networking activities and may be fined a maximum of 15,000 yuan (US$1,800) by a public security organization, perhaps at the suggestion of other units in the industry.

Article 15: Violators of these regulations and other related laws and regulations will be penalized according to relevant laws and regulations; offences deemed criminal will be prosecuted.

Article 16: These regulations should be consulted when implementing the security, protection and management of CINs connecting to networks in the Hong Kong Special Administrative Region as well as to networks in Taiwan and Macao.

Article 17: These regulations go into effect on the day of promulgation, i.e., 1 February 1996.

ANNEX 2

PRC MEASURES ON THE REGULATION OF PUBLIC COMPUTER NETWORKS AND THE INTERNET[164]

Article 1: In order to strengthen regulation of China's public computer networks connecting to the Internet and encourage expansion of international information exchange, these regulations are being established according to the PRC Interim Provisions on the Regulation of Computer Networks and the Internet.

Article 2: China Public Computer Network (i.e. CHINANET) refers to the interconnecting network built, operated and managed by China's General Bureau of Posts and Telecommunications (GBPT). This network connects computers to the Internet and is responsible for general service.

Article 3: CHINANET is divided into network management centres and information service centres.

Article 4: Organizations serving as entry point units for CHINANET should meet the following qualifications:

---

[164]The "PRC Measures on the Regulation of Public Computer Networks and the Internet" was issued by the Ministry of Post and Telecommunications (MPT, predecessor of the Ministry of Information Industry) on 9 April 1996.

1. They must be legally established enterprises, institutions or organizations.
2. They must be equipped with a regional network made up of main computer terminals and online information terminals along with related network facilities.
3. They must have relevant technological and administrative staff.
4. They must have a sound set of systems and procedures that ensure safety, safeguard secrecy and protect technologies.
5. They must also obey laws and regulations of the country as well as requirements set up by the Ministry of Posts and Telecommunications (MPT).

Article 5:   Entry point units intending to be connected to CHINANET should obtain the approval of their supervisory unit or department before applying to the GBPT. At the time of application, they must supply information on system composition, scope of usage, number of main networked terminals, and domain names and site addresses along with end-user data. After the connection is made, changes in any of these areas should be reported in a timely manner to the GBPT.

Article 6:   Computers and other telecommunications terminals belonging to individuals, legal persons and other organizations (hereafter referred to as "users" in this document) must connect to the Internet through the entry point network. Users can use a special line or the public telecommunications exchange network to enter the entry point network.

Article 7:   GBPT is responsible for the management of networking between entry point units and users. It is also under obligation to provide high-performance, safe and reliable services to them.

Article 8:   Entry point units are responsible for the management of users they connect to the Internet. They should sign agreements with users, clearly outlining both parties' rights, duties and responsibilities.

Article 9:   Entry point units and users should obey the laws and regulations of the country, reinforce information security education, implement the country's regulations on securing classified information and assume responsibility for the information they provide.

Article 10: No unit or individual may use the Internet to engage in criminal activities such as harming national security or disclosing state secrets. No unit or individual may use the Internet to retrieve, replicate, create, or transmit information that harms national security, threatens social stability and promotes sexually suggestive material. Discoveries of the aforementioned criminal activities and harmful information should be reported to related supervisory units in a timely fashion.

Article 11: No unit or individual may use the Internet to engage in activities that harm other people's information systems and network security. No unit or individuals may use the Internet to engage in activities that infringe on other people's legal rights.

Article 12: Connecting network units, entry point units and users must co-operate with the state's legitimate efforts to monitor and inspect Internet information security, and they should provide necessary information and conditions.

Article 13:   Units that provide computer information services domestically by using Internet information sources must be inspected and approved by the regulations governing public telecommunications service providers.

Article 14:   Entry point units and users who violate Article 5 and/ or Article 6 by connecting to the Internet through CHINANET without proper authorization and permission will have their connecting services terminated by the GBPT. In more serious cases, punishment will be sought from public security organizations.

Article 15:   Violators of Articles 9, 10 and 11 will be penalized by warnings from the MPT or the postal and telecommunications regulatory bureau (PTRB), followed by the revocation of approval documents, and finally by notices to the public telecommuncations enterprise to terminate the networking activity of the violators. For more serious offenses, the matter will be turned over to public security organizations. Any activities deemed criminal will be prosecuted.

Article 16:   Violations of Article 13 will be punished according to related regulations of the MPT or the PTRB.

Article 17:   These regulations go into effect on the day of promulgation, i.e., 9 April 1996.

ANNEX 3

COMPUTER INFORMATION NETWORK AND INTERNET SECURITY, PROTECTION AND MANAGEMENT REGULATIONS[165]

Chapter 1 Comprehensive Regulations

Article 1: In order to strengthen the security and the protection of computer information networks and of the Internet, and to preserve the social order and social stability, these regulations have been established on the basis of the "PRC Computer Information Network Protection Regulations", the "PRC Temporary Regulations on Computer Information Networks and the Internet" and other laws and administrative regulations.

Article 2: The security, protection and management of all computer information networks within the borders of the PRC fall under these regulations.

Article 3: The computer management and supervision organization of the Ministry of Public Security is

---

[165]The "Computer Information Network and Internet Security, Protection and Management Regulations" were approved by the State Council on 11 December 1997 and promulgated by the Ministry of Public Security on 30 December 1997. Source: "Computer Information Network and Internet Security, Protection and Management Regulations", *ChinaOnline*, http://www.chinaonline.com.

responsible for the security, protection and management of computer information networks and the Internet. The Computer Management and Supervision organization of the Ministry of Public Security should protect the public security of computer information networks and the Internet, the legal rights of Internet service providing units and individuals as well as the public interest.

Article 4:   No unit or individual may use the Internet to harm national security, disclose state secrets, harm the interests of the State, of society or of a group, the legal rights of citizens, or to take part in criminal activities.

Article 5:   No unit or individual may use the Internet to create, replicate, retrieve, or transmit the following kinds of information:

1. Inciting to resist or breaking the Constitution or laws or the implementation of administrative regulations;
2. Inciting to overthrow the government or the socialist system;
3. Inciting division of the country, harming national unification;
4. Inciting hatred or discrimination among nationalities or harming the unity of the nationalities;
5. Making falsehoods or distorting the truth, spreading rumours, destroying the order of society;
6. Promoting feudal superstitions, sexually suggestive material, gambling, violence, murder;
7. Terrorism or inciting others to criminal activity; openly insulting other people or distorting the truth to slander people;

8. Injuring the reputation of state organs; and
9. Other activities against the Constitution, laws or administrative regulations.

Article 6: No unit or individual may engage in the following activities, which harm the security of computer information networks:

1. No one may use computer networks or network resources without getting proper prior approval.
2. No one may without prior permission change network functions or add or delete information.
3. No one may without prior permission add to, delete, or alter materials stored, processed or being transmitted through the network.
4. No one may deliberately create or transmit viruses.
5. Other activities that harm the network are also prohibited.

Article 7: The freedom and privacy of network users is protected by law. No unit or individual may, in violation of these regulations, use the Internet to violate the freedom and privacy of network users.

Chapter 2 Responsibility for Security and Protection

Article 8: Units and individuals engaged in Internet business must accept the security supervision, inspection, and guidance of the Public Security organization. This includes providing to the Public Security organization information, materials and digital document, and assisting the Public Security organization to discover and properly handle incidents involving law violations and criminal activities involving computer information networks.

Article 9: The supervisory section or supervisory units of units which provide service through information network gateways through which information is imported and exported and connecting network units should, according to the law and relevant state regulations, assume responsibility for the Internet network gateways as well as the security, protection, and management of the subordinate networks.

Article 10: Connecting network units, entry point units and corporations that use computer information networks and the Internet and other organizations must assume the following responsibilities for network security and protection:

1. Assume responsibility for network security, protection and management and establish a thoroughly secure, protected and well-managed network.
2. Carry out technical measures for network security and protection. Ensure network operational security and information security.
3. Assume responsibility for the security education and training of network users.
4. Register units and individuals to whom information is provided. Provide information according to the stipulations of Article 5.
5. Establish a system for registering the users of electronic bulletin board systems on the computer information network as well as a system for managing bulletin board information.

6. If a violation of Articles 4, 5, 6 or 7 is discovered then an unaltered record of the violation should be kept and reported to the local Public Security organization.

7. According to the relevant State regulations, remove from the network and address, directory or server, which has content in violation of Article 5.

Article 11: The network user should fill out a user application form when applying for network services. The format of this application form is determined by the Public Security.

Article 12: Connecting network units, entry point units, and corporations that use computer information networks and the Internet and other organizations (including connecting network units that are inter-provincial, autonomous region, municipalities directly under the Central Government or the branch organization of these units) should, within 30 days of the opening of network connection, carry out the proper registration procedures with a unit designated by the Public Security organization of the provincial, autonomous region, or municipality directly under the Central Government peoples' government.

The units mentioned above have the responsibility to report for the record to the local Public Security organization information on the units and individuals which have connections to the network. The units must also report in a timely manner to the Public Security organization any changes in the information about units or individuals using the network.

Article 13:   People who register public accounts should strengthen their management of the account and establish an account registration system. Accounts may not be lent or transferred.

Article 14:   Whenever units involved in matters such as national affairs, economic construction, building the national defence, and advanced science and technology are registered, evidence of the approval of the chief administrative section should be shown.

Appropriate measures should be taken to ensure the security and protection of the computer information network and Internet network links of the units mentioned above.

Chapter 3 Security and Supervision

Article 15:   The provincial, autonomous region or municipal Public Security agency or bureau, as well as city and county Public Security organizations should have appropriate organizations to ensure the security, protection and management of the Internet.

Article 16:   The Public Security organization computer management and supervision organization should have information on the connecting network units, entry point unit, and users, establish a filing system for this information, maintain statistical information on these files and report to higher level units as appropriate.

Article 17:   The Public Security computer management and supervision organization should have established a system for ensuring the security, protection and good management of the connecting network units, entry point unit, and users. The Public Security organization should supervise and inspect network security, protection and management and the implementation of security measures.

Article 18: If the Public Security computer management and supervision organization discovers an address, directory or server with content in violation of Article 5, then the appropriate units should be notified to close or delete it.

Article 19: The Public Security computer management and supervision organization is responsible for pursuing and dealing with illegal computer information network activities and criminal cases involving computer information networks. Criminal activities in violation of Article 4 or Article 7 should, according to the relevant state regulations, be handed over to the relevant department or to the legal system for appropriate disposition.

Chapter 4 Legal Responsibility

Article 20: For violations of law, administrative regulations or of Article 5 or Article 6 of these regulations, the Public Security organization gives a warning and if there is income from illegal activities, confiscates the illegal earnings.

For less serious offences, a fine not exceeding 5000 yuan on individuals and 15,000 yuan on work units may be imposed.

For more serious offences, computer and network access can be closed down for six months; and, if necessary, the Public Security can suggest the cancellation of the business operating license of the concerned unit or of its network registration. Management activities that constitute a threat to public order can be punished according to provisions of the public security management penalty articles. Where crimes have occurred, prosecutions for criminal responsibility should be made.

Article 21: Where one of the activities listed below has occurred, the Public Security organization should order that remedial action be taken within a specific period and a warning given; if there has been illegal income, the income should be confiscated; if remedial action is not taken within the specified period, then a fine of not more than 5000 yuan may be imposed against the head of the unit and any person directly under the unit head and a fine of not more than 15,000 yuan against the unit; in the case of more offences, the network and equipment can be closed for up to six months. In serious cases, the Public Security may suggest that the business license of the organization be cancelled and its network registration cancelled.

1. Not setting up a secure system;
2. Not implementing security techniques and protection measures;
3. Not providing security education and training for network users;
4. Not providing information, materials or electronic documentation needed for security, protection and management, or providing false information;

5. Not inspecting the content of information transmitted on behalf of someone else or not registering the unit or individual on whose behalf the information was transmitted;
6. Not establishing a system for registering users and managing the information of electronic bulletin boards;
7. Not removing web addresses and directories or not closing servers according to the relevant state regulations;
8. Not establishing a system for registering users of public accounts; and
9. Lending or transferring accounts.

Article 22: Violation of Articles 4 or 7 of these regulations shall be punished according to the relevant laws and regulations.

Article 23: Violations of Articles 11 or 12 of these regulations or not fulfilling the responsibility or registering users shall be punished by a warning from the Public Security or suspending network operations for six months.

Chapter 5 Additional Regulations

Article 24: These regulations should be consulted with regards to the implementation of the security, protection and management of computer information networks connecting to networks in the Hong Kong Special Administrative Region as well as with networks in the Taiwan and Macao districts.

Article 25: These regulations go into effect on the day of promulgation, i.e., 30 December 1997.

ANNEX 4

STATE SECRECY PROTECTION REGULATIONS FOR COMPUTER INFORMATION SYSTEMS ON THE INTERNET[166]

Chapter 1 General Principles

Article 1: These Regulations are issued in line with the "Law of the People's Republic of China on the Protection of State Secrets" and other related regulations of China to strengthen the management of secrets for the computer systems on the Internet and to ensure the safety of state secrets.

Article 2: Computer systems on the Internet refers to the connection of computer information systems within the territory of the People's Republic of China with foreign computer information networks to achieve the international exchange of information.

Article 3: All individuals, corporations and other organizations (hereafter collectively referred to as "users"), national

[166]The "State Secrecy Protection Regulations for Computer Information Systems on the Internet" was issued by the Bureau for the Protection of State Secrets (State Secrets Bureau) on 25 January 2000. Source: "State Secrecy Protection Regulations for Computer Information Systems on the Internet", *ChinaOnline*, http://www.chinaonline.com.

backbone networks and Internet access providers using international networking shall abide by these Regulations.

Article 4: The management of secrets for the computer systems on the Internet is based on the principles of controlling sources, centralized management by corresponding departments, responsibility at different levels, emphasizing key points and benefiting development.

Article 5: State departments in charge the protection of secrets shall take charge of protecting secrets for national computer information systems on the Internet. Local departments for the protection of secrets above the county level shall take charge of the work concerning the computer systems on the Internet within their respective administrative districts. Central government institutions, in the area of their functions and powers, shall take charge of or guide the work of guarding secrets for the computer systems on the Internet within their own systems.

Chapter 2 Security Mechanism

Article 6: A computer information system involving state secrets shall not be connected, either directly or indirectly, with the Internet or other public information networks. It must be physically separated.

Article 7: Information involving state secrets, including information that has been checked and authorized to be legally exchanged, in instances of foreign exchanges and Cupertino, through special equipment outside

China's territory, shall not be stored, processed and transmitted in computer information systems with Internet connection.

Article 8:   The management of secrets concerning information on the Internet shall be based on the principle of "whoever places materials on the Internet takes the responsibility". Information provided to or released on Websites must undergo a security inspection and approval. And inspection and approval should be carried out by related departments, related units shall, in line with state laws and regulations on guarding secrets, establish and improve a leadership responsibility system for the examination and approval of information intended for the Internet. Units that provide the information shall establish a security system for information examination and approval in accordance with certain work procedures.

Article 9:   As for information collected for the purpose of providing Internet information services, not including what has been published by other news media, hosts shall obtain the approval of the units providing the information before releasing it on the Internet. Any expansion or updating of information on the Internet shall adhere strictly to the security system for information examination and approval.

Article 10:   Units and users that establish BBS, chatrooms or network newsgroups shall be verified and approved by the relevant organizations to clarify the requirements and responsibilities concerning the protection of secrets.

No unit or individual shall release, discuss or disseminate information about state secrets on BBS, chatrooms or network newsgroups.

For BBS, chatrooms or network newsgroups that are open to the public, the host or its higher level competent department shall strictly carry out its responsibilities concerning the protection of secrets, establish a complete management system and strengthen supervision and inspection. If information related to secrets is discovered, it shall take timely measures and report this to the local authorities for the protection of secrets.

Article 11: Users who exchange information on the Internet via email shall abide by regulations concerning the guarding of state secrets. They shall not deliver, forward or copy information concerning state secrets via email.

National backbone networks and Internet access providers shall clarify to their email users their requirements for protecting secrets and shall improve their management systems.

Article 12: National backbone networks and Internet access providers shall provide instruction about protecting secrets as an important part of the Internet related technical training. Agreements and user rules signed between national backbone networks and Internet access providers, and between Internet access providers and users shall stipulate clearly that state laws on protecting secrets must be obeyed and that state secrets shall not be leaked.

Chapter 3 Supervising the Protection of Secrets

Article 13: Departments for protecting secrets at all levels shall have related organizations or personnel who are responsible for managing secrets for computer information systems on the Internet. They shall urge national backbone networks, Internet access providers and users to establish and complete a management system on the protection of secret information, and shall supervise and inspect the implementation of regulations concerning the protection of secrets on the Internet.

Departments or units that fail to establish a management system for protecting secrets, to stipulate clear-cut responsibilities or to take effective measures against chaotic management and hidden perils that evidently threaten the information security of state secrets, shall rectify these at the urging of authorities for the protection of secrets. Those departments or units that cannot meet the requirements for protecting secrets after the rectification is completed shall be urged to stop their Internet connections.

Article 14: Departments in charge of protecting secrets at all levels shall strengthen their inspections for secrets in computer information systems on the Internet. They shall investigate and treat various actions concerning leaks of secrets according to the law.

Article 15: National backbone networks, Internet access providers and users shall accept the supervision and inspection conducted by departments in charge of protecting secrets and shall co-operate with them. They shall assist secret-protection departments in investigating illegal actions that divulge state secrets on the Internet. They shall also delete information on the Internet that concerns state secrets, as required by the departments in charge of protecting secrets.

Article 16: When a leak, or possible leak, of state secrets is discovered, national backbone networks, Internet access providers and users shall immediately report this to the departments or organizations in charge of protecting secrets.

Article 17: After receiving a report on or discovering a leak of secrets on the Internet, the departments and organizations in charge of protecting secrets shall immediately organize an investigation and urge the relevant units to take remedial measures. Meanwhile, they shall supervise the relevant units' deletion within a stipulated period.

Chapter 4 Supplementary Provisions

Article 18: The management of secrets for computer information systems connecting with the Hong Kong and Macau Special Administrative Regions and Taiwan shall be carried out with reference to these Regulations.

Article 19: Specific rules may be made in conformity with these Regulations for managing secrets for military computer information systems on the Internet.

Article 20: These Regulations take effect on 1 January 2000.

ANNEX 5

RULES OF SHANGHAI MUNICIPALITY ON THE MANAGEMENT OF COMPUTER PUBLIC INFORMATION NETWORKS INVOLVING PERSONNEL EXCHANGE SERVICES

The Shanghai Personnel Bureau and the Office of the Shanghai Municipal Leading Group for National Economy and Social Information Technology Development (hereafter the Municipal IT Office) issued jointly on February 2000 the following "Rules of Shanghai Municipality on the Management of Computer Public Information Networks Involving Personnel Exchange Services". These regulations took effect on 1 April 2000.

Article 1: Objectives and Bases

These rules were formulated in accordance with the "Regulations of Shanghai Municipality on the Mobility of Talented Personnel". They seek to standardize activities of personnel exchange services by means of computer public information networks, to ensure the legal rights and interests of parties involved in the personnel exchange, and to promote the healthy development of personnel exchange services as well as computer public information services.

Article 2: Scope of Application

These rules apply to personnel exchange services and the release of information on personnel exchanges by means of computer public information networks, as well as corresponding management activities, within the Shanghai municipal administrative division.

Article 3: Regulatory Entities

The Municipal IT Office is the competent authority for the administration of the city's computer public information networks. The Shanghai Personnel Bureau (or Municipal Personnel Bureau) is the competent authority for the city's flow of talented personnel. The Municipal IT Office and the Municipal Personnel Bureau exercise supervision and administration over activities involving personnel exchanges by means of computer public information networks within the Shanghai municipal administrative division.

District and county IT development organizations and district and county personnel bureaus shall, under the guidance of the Municipal IT Office and the Municipal Personnel Bureau, respectively, exercise supervision and administration over activities involving personnel exchange by means of computer public information networks within their respective administrative division.

Article 4: Qualifications

Institutions for personnel exchange services possessing a License of the Shanghai Municipality for Personnel Exchange Services, and which engage in intermediary services of personnel exchange by means of computer public information networks, shall, in accordance with the "Announcement of Shanghai Municipality on Strengthening the Business Examination and Registration of Computer Public Information Services", apply to the municipal, district or county IT office for a Permit of Shanghai Municipality for Computer Public Information Services.

Institutions of personnel services possessing a License of the Shanghai Municipality for Personnel Exchange Services, which authorizes institutions of computer public information services to release their intermediary service information on personnel exchanges online, may be exempted from applying for a Permit of Shanghai Municipality for Computer Public Information Services.

Institutions of computer public information services possessing a Permit of Shanghai Municipality for Computer Public Information Services, and which engage in the part-time online business of intermediary services for personnel exchanges, shall, in accordance with the "Implementing Rules of Shanghai Municipality on Strengthening the Management of Personnel Exchange Service Institutions", apply to the municipal, district or county personnel bureau for a License of the Shanghai Municipality for Personnel Exchange Services.

Institutions of computer public information services possessing a Permit of Shanghai Municipality for Computer Public Information Services, and which act as agents to release information on personnel exchanges and which do not engage in the part-time online business of intermediary services on personnel exchanges, may be exempted from applying for a License of the Shanghai Municipality for Personnel Exchange Services.

Article 5: Information Verification

The contents of information on personnel exchange to be released on computer public information networks shall be submitted to the agencies authorized by the municipal, district or county personnel bureau for examination and approval.

Article 6: Truthfulness of Information

Information on personnel exchanges shall be accurate and abide by related laws and regulations. Providers of information on personnel exchanges shall not provide false information.

Article 7: Administrative Measures

For actions violating the first clause of Article 4 of the Rules, the Municipal IT Office may circulate a notice of criticism and compel correction within a prescribed time.

For actions transgressing the third clause of Article 4, Article 5 or Article 6, the municipal, district or county personnel bureau may circulate a notice of criticism and compel correction within a prescribed time.

Other actions that violate related regulations of the state and the municipality shall be dealt with accordingly.

Article 8: Interpretation Authorities

The Municipal IT Office and the Municipal Personnel Bureau are responsible for interpreting the Rules.

Article 9: Date of Implementation

The Rules took effect from 1 April 2000.

ANNEX 6

REGULATIONS ON THE REGISTRATION AND FILING OF ONLINE BUSINESS OPERATIONS

The Regulations on the Registration and Filing of Online Business Operations, which were issued by the Beijing Municipal Administration for Industry and Commerce, took effect on 1 September 2000.[167]

Chapter 1 General Provisions

Article 1:   These Procedures are made in accordance with related state laws and regulations in a bid to protect the legitimate rights and interests of business website owners and standardize the operation of Web sites.

Article 2:   Procedures for the filing and registration of business websites are identical throughout the country. The Beijing Municipal Administration for Industry and Commerce, as the competent authority authorized by the State Administration for Industry and Commerce for experimenting with the national filing and registration of business websites (referred to as the

---

[167]"China Posts New Business Website Regulations", *Chinaonline* (12 September 2000), http://www.chinaonline.com.

Competent Authority hereafter), exercises supervision and management over business websites.

Article 3: A business website in these Procedures is defined as an electronic platform established with Internet technologies and with an independent domain name obtained from the domain name authorities. Through this platform, the owner of the website can release information and advertisements, set up e-mail boxes and conduct business activities via the Internet, or provide Internet space to others for carrying out the aforesaid activities.

The owner of the website refers to the owner of the domain name of the website, except what is stipulated in a contract.

Article 4: A business website in these Procedures is a website with one of the following features:

1. The owner of the website or one of the owners of the website is an enterprise; or
2. The website engages in business operations aiming to make a profit.

Article 5: An owner of a business website shall apply to the Competent Authority for filing and registration, obtain a Certificate of Business Website Filed and Registered, and install electronic identification for filing and registration on the front page of the site. The Beijing Municipal Administration for Industry and Commerce itself makes the paper copies of the certificate as well as the electronic identification.

Article 6:   The owner of a business website shall provide personnel for information checks to prevent and eliminate, in a timely manner, all kinds of unlawful information or information that harms social morals and efforts to build a socialist civilization with a high cultural and ideological level.

Article 7:   While operating a website, the owner of a business website shall abide by state laws and regulations, adhere to professional ethics, raise the level of socialist civilization, improve internal management, accept supervision from the government and pubic alike, and prevent illegal operations.

Chapter 2 Application, Verification and Ratification

Article 8:   The establishment of a business website is handled as the establishment of a branch of an enterprise. If explicit stipulations are made in these Procedures concerning specific matters, such provisions shall be followed.

Article 9:   The filing and registration of a business website shall be applied for by the owner of the site. If the owner of a website entrusts the filing and registration to others, the filing and registration shall be carried out in accordance with regulations of the Competent Authority.

Article 10:   The owner of a business website shall have a relevant business scope. If a business website was opened prior to the promulgation of these Procedures and does not conform to the previous provision, its owner shall go through formalities at the local administration for industry and commerce and rectify the business scope within 30 days beginning from the day of the promulgation of these Procedures.

Article 11:   Individuals that establish a business website shall go through related formalities for industrial and commercial registration and obtain a business license before applying for the filing and registration of the website.

Individuals who opened a business website prior to the promulgation of the Procedures shall go through the aforesaid formalities at the local administration for industry and commerce.

Article 12:   The filing and registration of a business website shall include information on the basic conditions of the website and the owner of the website. The owner of the website shall, according to the requirements of the Competent Authority, accurately fill out and submit relevant documents and testimonial papers.

Article 13:   While going through formalities of filing and registration, the business website shall apply for the registration of its domain name.

Article 14:   The application, obtaining, modification, cancellation and other issues relating to the name of the website shall be dealt with by the Competent Authority in line with related provisions in the Interim Procedures Governing the Registration of Website Names and detailed rules for their implementation.

Article 15:   The applicant shall apply for the filing and registration of websites online and submit relevant information in conformity with the forms and procedures provided at the website of Hongdun 315.

Article 16: The applicant shall submit written testimonial documents to the Competent Authority within 30 days of completing the online application. If the applicant fails to submit the written testimonial documents within the stated period of time, the application shall be cancelled.

Article 17: After ratifying the application documents submitted by the owner of a website, the Competent Authority shall guide the owner of the website to download and install electronic identification. Only when the electronic identification is correctly installed can the website start trial operation.

Article 18: During trial operation, the Competent Authority shall announce the name of the registered website in accordance with the Interim Procedures Governing the Registration of Website Names.

During trial operation, the name of the registered website is subject to dispute. During the period, the owner of the website shall have no exclusive right to the name of the website being used.

Article 19: The Competent Authority will issue a Certificate of Website Name Registered and a Certificate of Business Website Filed and Registered to the Website upon ratification of its registered name. The Competent Authority shall also issue a public notice. From then on, the owner of the website has the exclusive right to the name of the registered website and the site automatically begins formal operation.

Article 20: If the website does not pass the period of dispute on the name of the registered website, the owner of the website may re-apply for the name of registered website. During the re-application, the period of dispute will be postponed. The continuous time of the trial operation of a business website shall be no more than 12 months.

Chapter 3 Modification, Assignment and Annual Checks

Article 21: If any modification is to be made in the filing and registration of the business website, the owner of a website shall, according to related regulations, apply to the Competent Authority to make changes relating to the filing and registration. Name changes of a website shall accord with related provisions as stipulated in the Interim Procedures Governing the Registration of Website Names.

Article 22: If a business website is to be transferred, the transferor shall apply for cancellation and submit the letter of assignment reached by the two parties. Upon approval of the Competent Authority, the transferor no longer has the relevant rights for online operation or the exclusive rights to the name of the registered website. The Competent Authority revokes the Certificate of WebSite Name Registered and the Certificate of Business Website Filed and Registered from the transferor.

Article 23: The assignee shall apply to the Competent Authority for filing and registration according to the Procedures. Upon confirmation, the Competent Authority issues the Certificate of Website Name Registered and the

Certificate of Business Website Filed and Registered and makes an announcement.

Article 24: After obtaining a Certificate of Business Website Filed and Registered, a business website shall apply to the Competent Authority for annual checks. In the meantime, the site shall apply to the Competent Authority for any modifications to be made in the registration.

Chapter 4 Cancellation

Article 25: If a website stops operation because it is closed, revoked, or bankrupt or for other reasons, the owner of the website shall go through cancellation formalities at the Competent Authority.

Article 26: While going through cancellation formalities, the owner of the website shall provide the Competent Authority with an application form for cancelling the registration and other related testimonial documents. Upon ratification, the Competent Authority shall take back the Certificate of Website Name Registered and the Certificate of Business Website Filed and Registered and revoke the electronic identification.

Chapter 5 Supervision and Management

Article 27: If a website fails to operate within six months after its owner obtains a Certificate of Business Website Filed and Registered, or if the website stops operation for one year, the Competent Authority shall take back the Certificate of Website Name Registered and the

Certificate of Business Website Filed and Registered and shall revoke the electronic identification.

Article 28: The Competent Authority shall, according to related laws and regulations, mete out penalties to those violating Article 10 and Article 11 of the Procedures.

Article 29: In any one of the following cases, the Competent Authority may order the owner of a website to amend its behaviour. If the misconduct is of a serious nature, the Competent Authority can revoke the Certificate of Business Website Filed and Registered as well as the electronic identification and make an announcement. Misconduct of a serious nature includes:

- Concealing the true facts and practising fraud in the filing and registration;
- Forging, obliterating, renting, lending, selling or arbitrarily assigning a Certificate of Business Website Filed and Registered;
- Installing the electronic identification incorrectly and refusing to correct it, or arbitrarily changing the electronic identification;
- Not cancelling the registration or conducting annual checks in accordance with stipulated provisions; and
- Engaging in illegal activity on the filed and registered website.

Article 30: Websites which were set up and did not going through formalities of filing and registration prior to the promulgation of the Procedures, shall file and register with the Competent Authority within 60 days after the promulgation of the Procedures. Administrations for industry and commerce shall order those that fail to go through the formalities within the stated time to correct themselves. Activities of a serious nature shall be investigated and penalized in accordance with administrative regulations governing industry and commerce.

Article 31: Website owners that forge the electronic identification shall be investigated and penalized by administrations for industry and commerce in line with related laws and regulations.

Chapter 6 Supplementary Provisions

Article 32: Websites that filed and registered for online operations prior to the promulgation of the Procedures shall update their formalities in accordance with related provisions at the site of Hongdun 315.

Article 33: Beijing Municipal Administration for Industry and Commerce shall be responsible for interpretation of the Procedures.

Article 34: These Procedures took effect on 1 September 2000.

The Announcement of Beijing Municipal Administration for Industry and Commerce on the Registration and Filing of Online Business Operations issued on 28 March 2000, and its supplementary rules issued on 18 May 2000, shall be simultaneously abolished.

ANNEX 7

GUIDELINES ON THE DEVELOPMENT OF CHINA'S E-COMMERCE INDUSTRY

In December 1999, the Ministry of Information Industry issued several guidelines on the development of China's e-commerce industry:[168]

i. E-commerce must serve the national economy and "should conform to China's unique set of circumstances".

ii. The government will manage the development of e-commerce in China. "Government agencies must ensure that all policies, regulations and standards are uniform."

iii. Enterprises will be "encouraged to participate in the development of e-commerce" in China.

iv. "Model e-commerce businesses will be launched to stimulate the proliferation of ecommerce in China."

v. Laws, regulations and security procedures will be established for the sake of national security. "Government agencies have the responsibility to monitor and regulate core security technologies."

vi. International e-commerce is to be "actively pursued". The government should establish a legal environment that is suitable for China and "fits in the global scheme of things".

---

[168]"MII Wants Ecommerce Development With Chinese Characteristics", *Chinaonline* (22 December 1999) http://www.chinaonline.com.

ANNEX 8

CIRCULAR OF THE BEIJING MUNICIPAL ADMINISTRATION FOR INDUSTRY AND COMMERCE CONCERNING E-COMMERCE ACTIVITIES REGISTRATION

The "Circular of the Beijing Municipal Administration for Industry and Commerce Concerning E-commerce Activities Registration" was issued by the Beijing Municipal Administration for Industry and Commerce on 28 March 2000. This circular was formulated to meet the requirements of China's Internet economic development, namely, to differentiate and standardize business activities on the Internet, to enhance government's sense of service, to protect the lawful rights and interests of enterprises and consumers, to crack down on illegal business activities, to maintain the socioeconomic order and to establish an e-commerce operations registration system.

I. E-commerce activities refer to profit-making activities on the Internet of market subjects within the jurisdiction of Beijing municipality which have obtained a business license in accordance with state laws (hereafter referred to as "e-commerce dealers"), as well as the acts of image designing, product publication, auctions and advertising for economic organizations. E-commerce dealers engaged in the following activities should apply for an e-commerce operations registration:

1. Signing contracts, doing business and trading on the Internet;
2. Releasing commercial advertisements on the Internet;
3. Carrying out image designing and product publication activities on the Internet;
4. Specializing in providing Internet-access service, network technical support service, e-commerce and information source service on the Internet; and
5. Other profit-making activities.

II. The Beijing Municipal Administration for Industry and Commerce is the registering office for e-commerce operations. E-commerce dealers should apply to register their e-commerce operations at http://hd315.com, which was established by the Beijing Municipal Administration for Industry and Commerce.

III. The major types of information needed to register include: the type of e-commerce involved, the name of the e-commerce dealer, the registration number (or the number of a valid certificate), location (family address), legal representative, registered capital, type, business scope, the person in charge of the network management, network business scope, mailing address, telephone number, email address, registered domain name, Internet protocol address and network supplier, network address, name and location of the server, and other information.

IV. After the registration office receives the application of an e-commerce dealer, the office will complete the registration online, and, meanwhile, arrange the coding of the registration and provide a registration seal via the Internet. The e-commerce dealer should then post this registration seal on the homepage of its website.

V. Where changes occur in the major registration information, the e-commerce dealer should apply to the registry office to update these, and the registry office should change the related registration after receiving the updated application.

VI. Where an e-commerce dealer wants to cancel or stop its business operations, the said dealer should apply to the registry office to remove its registration. The registry office, after receiving the application, should withdraw its network sign. If the statutory qualification of an e-commerce dealer is revoked according to the law, the registry office has the power to terminate its registration and to withdraw the network sign.

VII. E-commerce dealers who have already completed the registration of their e-commerce operations are still required to obtain lawful business qualifications before beginning actual commercial operations.

VIII. There shall be no charge to register to carry out e-commerce operations.

IX. E-commerce dealers shall be subject to the supervision of the registry office in accordance with state laws, regulations and the provisions of these rules. The registry office exercises supervision over the activities of e-commerce dealers according to the law and punishes lawbreakers in accordance with the relevant laws and administrative regulations.

X. As for e-commerce operations in existence prior to the release of this circular, the party concerned should apply to the registry office within 180 days after this circular is issued.

ANNEX 9

NEW RULES ON E-COMMERCE DIGITAL CERTIFICATES

The new rules on digital certificates as provided in the Provisional Methods Of Shanghai Municipality On The Price Management of E-commerce was published on 4 April 2000.

Article 1: Basis And Objectives

The Methods are made in accordance with the Price Law of the People's Republic of China, the Regulations of Shanghai Municipality on Price Management and other relevant laws, regulations and provisions while taking into account the reality of Shanghai Municipality.

The purpose is to strengthen management of the pricing of e-commerce digital certificate (hereafter referred to as digital certificates) authentication and to standardize service charges in relation to the authentication of digital certificates.

Article 2: Scope Of Application

Applications for and the issuing, verification, management and use of digital certificates and related administration activities within the Shanghai administrative division shall abide by the Methods.

Article 3: Administrative Departments

Shanghai National Economy and Social Informization Leading Group Office (hereafter referred to as the Info Office) is the competent administrative department for authenticating digital certificates in the city.

The Shanghai Price Bureau (hereafter referred to as the Price Bureau) is the competent administrative department in charge of pricing in relation to digital certificates in the city.

Article 4: Digital Certificate Authentication Authority

The Shanghai Electronic Certificate Authority Center Co., Ltd. (hereafter referred to as the CA Center) is the only institution responsible for the issuing, verification and management of digital certificates in Shanghai. The CA Center can entrust related units with the acceptance and issuing of digital certificates.

Article 5: Services

Services concerning the issuing, verification and management of digital certificates include:

1. Opening new accounts: Services include customer identity verification, digital certificate creation, certificate storage, certificate management, certificate inquiry, regular certificate maintenance, certificate instalment and guidance for use.
2. Certificate renewal: The renewal of certificates shall occur in the original storage medium. Except for the verification of customer identity, other services are identical with the application for opening an account.
3. Reporting the loss of certificates: Service consists of entering the invalid certificate in the blacklist database.
4. Information requests: information support is provided to users of digital certificates.

5. Technical appraisal: Services are provided in relation to technical appraisal and proof of digital certificate and digital signature.
6. Special services: Services include cipher key entrustment, cipher key renewal, related software development, security system development, e-commerce consulting and technical guidance.

Article 6: Customer Rights

The issuing, verification and management of digital certificates are provided for a fee. Customers who pay the fees have the right to the corresponding services stipulated in Article 5 in the Methods.

Article 7: Form of Price Management

Fees for services such as application processing, certificate renewal, reporting certificate loss, information requests and technical appraisal are fixed by the government. Fees for special services are market-determined.

The Price Bureau and the Info Office are responsible for setting the government-fixed fees. The market price is determined through negotiations between the CA Center and customers on the principles of equality, free will, honesty and credit.

Article 8: Pricing Procedures

Concerning services whose fees are fixed by the government, the CA Center shall apply to the Info Office for the setting and adjustment of fees for the authentication of digital certificates. The CA Center shall also provide the cost and relevant data to the Info Office for examination and verification before submitting it to the Price Bureau for approval.

Concerning service fees for the issuing, verification and management of digital certificates, during the one-year trial period, the CA Center shall draft standards for service fees in line with related provisions in the Methods before submitting them to the Price Bureau and Info Office for recording.

Article 9: Fee Settlement

The renminbi is the currency in which service fees for the authentication of digital certificates are settled, and domestic and overseas settlements are handled separately. Domestic service fees for the authentication of digital certificates are settled in renminbi, while overseas service fees are settled in foreign currency based on the renminbi market exchange rate released by the State Administration of Foreign Exchange that day.

Article 10: Marked Prices

The CA Center and its business departments shall display the price list in a conspicuous spot at their business site. The prices shall be clearly marked to facilitate supervision and inspection by pricing authorities.

Article 11: Administrative Penalties

Pricing authorities shall penalize those who violate provisions in the Methods.

Article 12: Administrative Measures

The Info Office may circulate a notice of criticism concerning those violating provisions in the Methods and demand that violations be corrected within a stipulated time.

Article 13: Interpretation Authorities

The Price Bureau and the Info Office are responsible for interpreting the Methods.

Article 14: Date Of Enforcement

The Methods take effect as of 1 January 2000.